THE ART
of INLAY

THE ART of INLAY

Contemporary Design & Technique
for Musical Instruments, Fine Woodworking & Objets d'Art

BY LARRY ROBINSON
PHOTOGRAPHY BY RICHARD LLOYD

 Miller Freeman Books

SAN FRANCISCO 1999

Published by Miller Freeman Books,
600 Harrison Street, San Francisco, California 94107
Publishers of *Guitar Player, Bass Player,* and *Keyboard* magazines

Miller Freeman
A United News & Media publication

Distributed to the book trade in the U.S. and Canada by
Publishers Group West, 1700 Fourth Street, Berkeley, CA 94710

Distributed to the music trade in the U.S. and Canada by
Hal Leonard Publishing, P.O. Box 13819, Milwaukee, WI 53213

LIBRARY OF CONGRESS CATALOGING-IN-PUBLICATION DATA

Robinson, Larry, 1953–
    The art of inlay : contemporary design & technique / Larry Robionson
        p. cm.
    Includes bibliographical references.
    ISBN 0-87930-595-9
        1. Marquetry. 2. Musical instruments. 3. Decoration and ornament.
        I. Title.
    TT192.R65 1994
    749'.5—dc20

                                                                94-12076

Printed in the United States of America

99 00 01 02 03   5 4 3 2

Contents

To connie

WITHOUT WHOM MY LIFE WOULD BE BARE
AND THIS BOOK WOULDN'T EXIST

Foreword

I STARTED DOING FANCY INLAY WORK on electric instruments in 1968 or so, and one of my first commissions was a fingerboard on a custom Guild fretless bass for Phil Lesh of the Grateful Dead. This inlay job was my introduction to the Dead and led more or less directly to the formation of Alembic, Inc., in 1970. I think we were the first company to really make "art" electric instruments on any kind of regular basis, and to us the art included a nontraditional approach to inlay. Those were heady days, to be sure. We were building custom instruments for some of the top names in pop, rock, and jazz, and one of the things for which Alembic was known was fancy inlay work with a decidedly psychedelic twist.

Larry Robinson came to work for me at the infamous Alembic "Cotati chicken barn" guitar and bass factory in 1975, and he tells the story of his first inlay experience here in this book. Along with several other Alembic luthiers, Larry quickly became a remarkable inlay artist. Unlike the others, though, Larry has stuck with inlaying for nearly 20 years, specializing in the art and getting better and better with time.

Larry's work is remarkable on several accounts. First, his use of a wide palette of many different materials is outstanding. Traditional musical instrument inlays are general limited to just a few media—mother-of-pearl in its various guises, silver, ivory, and wood—and the media are very seldom combined and used together. Larry was never one to so restrict his options; one fingerboard may have all of those traditional materials augmented by copper, brass, bone, metal dust in superglue, turquoise, as well as anything else he can find around the house. Yes, I do believe he'd use the porcelain off the kitchen sink, if it matched the artistic need of the moment!

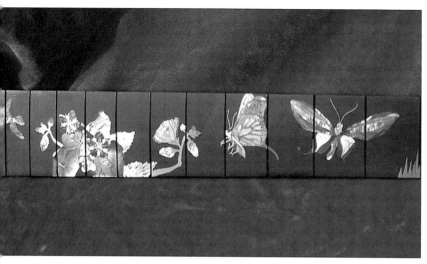

▲ Forest glade fingerboard inlay created by Larry Robinson for Rick Turner.

Then there is Larry's technique; I have never seen cleaner inlay work with less filler than his. I've seen some as good, but none better, and the good stuff is mostly from inlay artists who don't tackle the artistic or media challenges that Larry does. The first thing that inlay artists look for in someone else's work is the quality of the cutting and fitting. Larry's "chops" are simply world class, and in this book he generously lets you in on how he does it. Pay particular attention to his advice on layout and cutting.

Finally, there is Larry's artistry. He truly transcends materials and technique to become a pure artist. Larry once did a fingerboard for me that is a forest glade scene with a frog on a lily pad. Looking at that fingerboard, your eye fills in the whole scene beyond the physical borders of the instrument. You are in the forest, the frog is just about to jump, and you are ready to hear the splash! It's great inlay, but it's more than that; it's a great picture irrespective of the medium.

I am very proud to have had a hand in getting Larry started in this field. I feel like an old track coach whose athlete/protégé has just won a gold medal at the Olympics. Great book, Larry, and for all of you reading this, I hope you carry the art further on. Larry Robinson is just the guy to help you do it.

—Rick Turner
Topanga, California

♣ THE ART of INLAY

Acknowledgments

THERE ARE MANY PEOPLE responsible for putting a book together and bringing it to the attention of the general public. I will probably never meet some of the folks who funneled their energy and time into this project, but I'd like to thank them anyway.

First and foremost, Connie Campbell talked me into writing this book, then typed my original draft, untangling strangled syntax and generally making it easier to understand. This book is just as much hers as mine.

Richard Lloyd's photos, taken over a period of about ten years, make many of these pieces appear flawless. Thanks for the sleight-of-lens, Richard.

Thanks to everyone who read the first draft and offered constructive criticism, additions, and alternatives, especially Chuck Erikson (the Duke of Pearl) and Rick Turner.

Matt Kelsey, my editor/handler at Miller Freeman Books, deserves kudos for his patience and diplomatic finesse with first-time authors. George Mattingly should have more credit for the cover design, since that's what grabs people's attention first at the bookstore; and Fran Taylor, as copyeditor, fine-tuned the punctuation and will probably have readers believing that I was an English major in school, rather than the banal truth, which I will not divulge here.

I'm grateful to all the other inlay artists who submitted their slides for this project. There were a few of you whom I didn't know about before I got started, and I'm pleased to share these pages with you.

Finally, I'd like to thank the small army of publicists, printers, bosses, and hired guns who conspired to bring this little-known art to your attention.

▶ Lap desk.
PHOTO: RICHARD LLOYD.

Prologue

ICUT MY FIRST DECORATIVE INLAY in 1975 after I had been building guitars for three years. Having been trained in acoustic guitar construction, I thought that building electric solidbody guitars would be comparatively easy; so in my first week at Alembic, Inc., I managed to drill completely through two $2,000 basses while installing pickups.

While I mentally started looking for a new job, I called my boss, Rick Turner (the co-founder of Alembic, Inc.), over to the bench

◀ Drawing of Larry's first inlay

---

and showed him what I'd done. To my surprise and everlasting gratitude, he shrugged and said, "Just put an inlay over it. Then we can call it custom and charge more for it."

After he showed me the basics, I inlaid a hummingbird in one instrument, and some flowers over the damage in the other. I made more mistakes in the process, but fortunately none were as glaring as the original holes I was trying to cover.

Today inlaying is my business, and, although most of my work is subcontracted by other musical instrument manufacturers, I have other outlets, such as art galleries, jewelry stores, and craft fairs and exhibitions. Before I discuss techniques, here's a brief history of the art of inlay.

▶ Twelfth fret inlay.
PHOTO: RICHARD LLOYD.

♣ THE ART *of* INLAY

History

FIRST, I WOULD LIKE TO MAKE CLEAR that there is a difference between inlay and marquetry,* the latter being more prevalent in Western society, especially in furniture and the former in the Far East.

* Please consult the glossary, page 109, for definitions of unfamiliar terms.

Marquetry is the art of making patterns or pictures predominantly in wood veneers (but metal and shell have also been used) and gluing them directly *onto* the surface to be decorated. Inlay has traditionally been a composition of shell, metal, stone, and tusk (with wood to a lesser degree) that is glued *into* a cavity that has been hollowed out of the surface. The inlay is then sanded flush. Both techniques have their specialized tools and jargon, and, although some similarity between the two exists, this book will not deal with marquetry.

The earliest known inlaid object is a Mesopotamian limestone bowl with some shell pieces embedded in it, dated around 3000 BC. Another early example is a shell-inlaid wooden coffin from the Yin Dynasty (1300 BC–220 BC).

In the West the first inlays we know of appeared around 350 BC, and were done into marble. Later, during the Roman Empire, a method called *tarsia certosina* was developed, in which pieces of cut veneer were inlaid into cavities hewn into wood panels. After the fall of the Roman Empire this method fell into disuse as more crafts workers began developing the marquetry method of decoration.

In Nara, Japan, a series of 8th century storehouses is known as the Shoso-in Repository. The Emperor of Japan was an avid collector of artwork, and many pieces of inlaid art from the Repository still in pristine condition 1200 years later are held by experts to be unexcelled in design and construction.

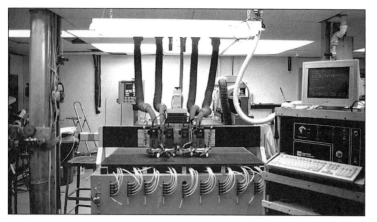

Pearl Works CAD-CAM operation.
LARRY SIFEL

The Asians also developed two distinct styles of inlay, only one of which is in common use in the West. Thick-shell inlay, known as *atsu-gai,* is inlaid into the surface of the wood. *Usu-gai,* or thin-shell inlay, is done with shell that is only around .005" thick and is cut into patterns with a knife or shaped punches and fixed directly onto a lacquer undercoat. The finish is then built up flush with the shell and buffed. Though many examples of finely wrought usu-gai pieces exist, and the materials are available from some shell suppliers, this book will deal mainly with the use of thicker stock (.03"–.06").

Contemporary American inlay most often appears on musical instruments. However, the market is evolving and examples can be found on signs, pool cue sticks, furniture, objets d'art, and along other more esoteric veins. Although the basic steps of construction involved have remained the same over centuries, the tools employed have kept up with high technology, at least in some cases. I know several people in the United States who use computer-controlled industrial-size vertical mills (CAD-CAM) equipped with multiple cutting heads specifically set up for inlaying. Programming the computer takes time and expertise, but cutting multiple images such as company logos or fingerboard positioning markers can be done in 30 seconds (on the average) instead of the half hour traditional methods would require.

Luckily for those of us who only do one-of-a-kind pieces, it's not cost-effective for computers to do our work.

How will this art develop in future years? If you're reading this book with the intent of learning how to inlay your own ideas, it's up to your imagination and perseverance. I hope I've been thorough enough in assembling this book so that you won't have to backtrack and redo things and don't develop bad work habits that are hard to break, as I have over the years.

Most of my knowledge of this craft has been the result of trial and error (and more error), as there were no books available on the subject. Over the years I've been fortunate enough to come to know a handful of people, true artists at inlay, who have been very generous with their time and hard-earned tips of the trade. For this I thank them profusely, especially Rick Turner, Chuck Erikson, Frank Fuller, Larry Sifel, Ren Ferguson, Dave Nichols, Richard Hoover, and Steve Klein.

▲ Larry Robinson's shop.

► Rosette on Joni Mitchell guitar. Designed by Mitchell, built by Steve Klein.

INLAYS BY LARRY ROBINSON

◄ An Art Deco resonator
for the Tsumura collection, 1991.

**(ALL PHOTOS IN THIS SECTION
ARE BY RICHARD LLOYD.)**

▶ Two of my electric guitars with symmetrical silver inlays in the necks. The six-string was built in 1976; the 12-string in 1978.

▼ Shell selection, clockwise from top: mother-of-pearl, black mother-of-pearl, green abalone, calcified clam, paua, brown lip, black abalone, gold mother-of-pearl. Center is red abalone.

✤ THE ART of INLAY

▼ (upper) Two Santa Cruz Guitar Co. pegheads, ca. 1991, with Celtic knot inlays, one in copper and abalone and one in mother-of-pearl and abalone.

▼ (lower) Twelfth fret of SCGC 12-string. Mother-of-pearl, gold mother-of-pearl, and engraved abalone.

"Fairies" theme for Triggs Guitars.
Various woods, metals, and shells.

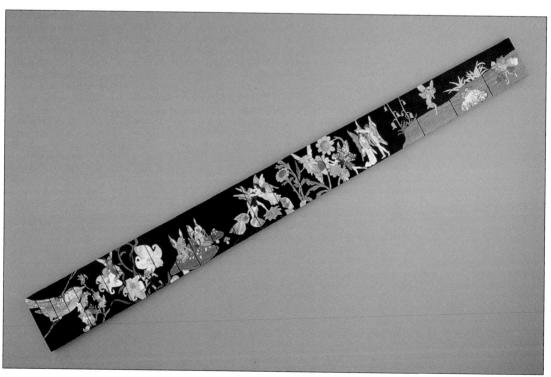

❧ THE ART of INLAY

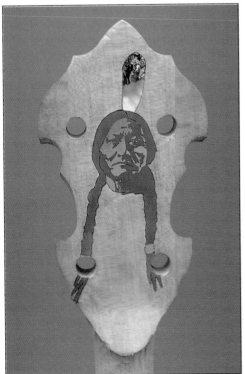

▲ "Custer's Last Stand" for Gibson Custom Shop, 1993.
Silver, brass, and copper silhouettes on fingerboard, various materials
on resonator and peghead.

◄ "Sitting Bull" on back of peghead is done in copper and silver,
feather in shell.

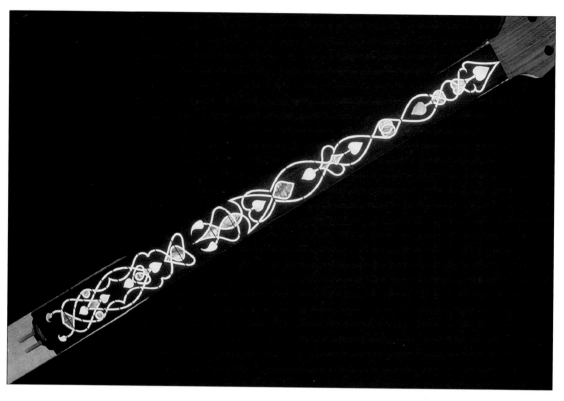

▲ Alembic neck for J. P. Jones of Led Zeppelin, early 1980s. Twelve gauge square silver stock with shell and ivory.

▶ Boxtop, 1985. Six-inch diameter. Dragon is wood, metal, ivory, and shell, laid into bloodwood.

♣ THE ART of INLAY

▼ Nineteenth century lap desk, restored by author in 1985.
Unfortunately, no "before" picture was taken, as the difference was quite startling.

► Kachina doll inlaid
into Osage orange slab, 1987.
Note the large piece of black
abalone heart in the skirt.

▼ Uncommissioned guitar built in 1988. I wanted to do this inlay for two years before I had the courage to attempt it, and I basically designed the guitar around the inlay, which is a copyrighted design by England's Roger Dean. All metal, except for the shell faceplate and tentacles drooping out of the "head." A red light-emitting diode (LED) buried beneath the faceplate lights up when the pickup preamp is turned on.

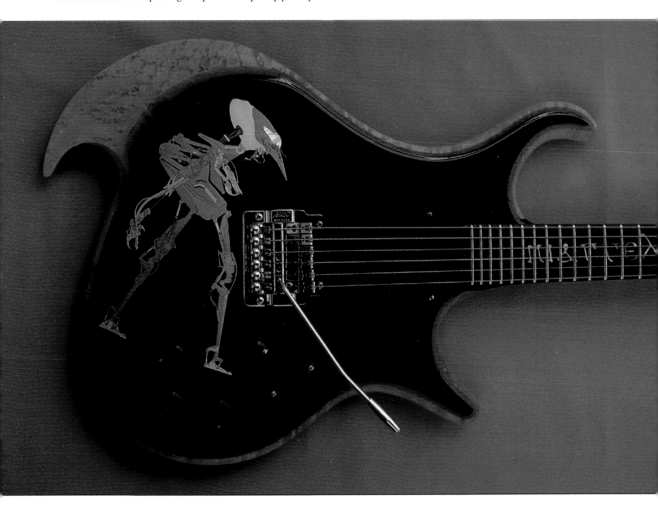

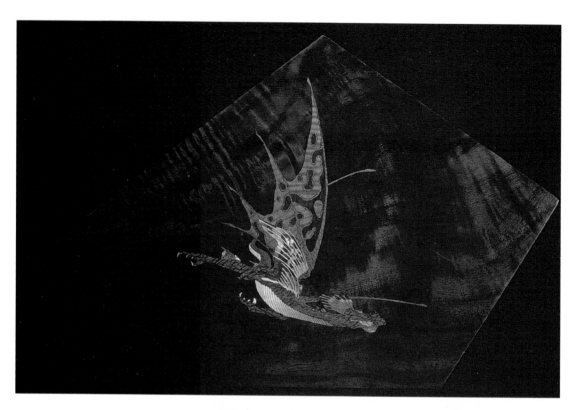

▲ Another Roger Dean design, copyright 1986. His Magnetic Storm Ltd. logo is embedded in California walnut. The entire mantle ornament is 19" long.

► The first Dean drawing I attempted, on my own jewelry box, 1979. (He copyrighted this design in 1975.) Note that all the scales were cut separately, so they would remain distinct, rather than being engraved on one large piece of abalone. This is inlaid into book-matched ebony sapwood, with just a bit of the heartwood down the center as a horizon line. The inlay is 8" long.

✣ THE ART of INLAY

◄ An 8" tall inlay I put on the back of my doubleneck guitar in 1984. From a drawing by Bernard and Barbara Xolotl, which graced Terry Riley's *Shri Camel* album. Lots of faceted gems sticking above the surface in this one. Inlaid into flamed redwood (kids, don't try this at home).

▲ Wolf head wall hanging inlaid in 2" thick walnut burl, ca. 1985. Silver, abalone, mother-of-pearl, and black mother-of-pearl, with alexandrite eyes that light up from red LEDs placed behind them. The head is about 7" tall.

▶ Triangle box of matched laurel, with 12-pointed Moroccan star in center. Three-and-three-quarter-inch inlay is copper, brass, silver, and red abalone heart.

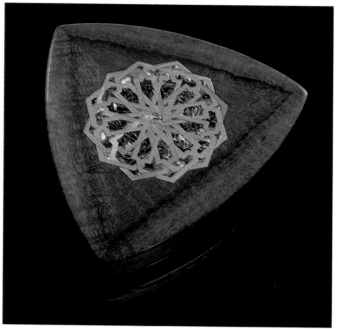

▼ Uncommissioned mantle ornament of a jaguar head, 1990.
The inlay is 10" tall, inlaid into the cutoff section of walnut from the Dean logo (top, page 26).
Copper, brass, abalone, and ebony with amber LEDs for eyes.

▲ Chinese octagon box of cocabolo, 1989. Houses eight different-colored pyramid-shaped quartz crystals. Five inches across.

❧ THE ART of INLAY

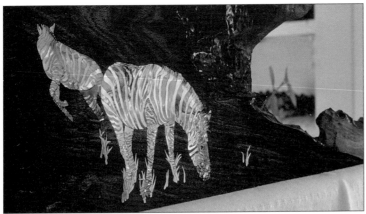

◄ Two zebras on Brazilian rosewood runout section, 1987. Red abalone and mother-of-pearl. Here's a great example of what happens to abalone when the light reflects from different angles.

▲ A new herd of zebras, 1993. Same materials as plates on previous page. Length is 26" overall.

Materials

O NE OF THE MOST pleasing aspects of inlaying is the variety of materials that can be used in the creative process. This same variety can also be quite frustrating at times. Apart from the often mind-boggling array of shell types, metals, woods (natural and dyed), stones, gems, bones, seven kinds of ivory, and vegetable nuts (tagua), there are enough different cuts, sections, grain patterns, refractive alignments, and chemical treatments affecting them to give the indecisive artist an anxiety attack.

Most of these possibilities are dealt with after the drawing is finished and before cutting begins, but some can assert themselves just before a final finish is put on the work. Some materials possess irregular characteristics that are not visible before the process of sanding the inlay level. This is usually the case with abalone shell, whose grain patterns change as it is sanded thinner.

▲ Various shell types.

I will now attempt to do justice to a physical description of the materials used in inlay, beginning with the shells.

If I had to describe the thousands of shell varieties and markings found on them, this could turn into a book the size of a telephone directory. Fortunately, commercial slabbing of shell for inlays is limited to a narrow range of species for a variety of reasons, among them Fish and Game regulations, as well as shell size, coloring, and curvature. Often the fantastic patterns seen on shell surfaces are only a few thousandths of an inch thick and, when sanded only a little, reveal a fairly uniform and boring interior. Many shells that do have attractive nacre inside are too thin walled or too heavily radiused to be worth cutting commercially. Sometimes if I need a particular color or shade, I'll obtain a certain shell and cut it up myself, but that is a rare occurrence.

Of the types of shell that can be cut into flat plates and large quantities, the most readily available are abalone (genus *Haliotis*) and mother-of-pearl (genus *Pinctada*). Abalones are fairly abundant in the Pacific Basin, but lately the supply has become more restricted and the shells harvested haven't been as large as they used to be, mostly due to overfishing, otter depredation, and "killer tides."

Abalones are gastropods, which translates to "stomach-foot" in plain English. They have only one arched shell over their body to protect them from predators and a suckerlike foot that attaches to rocks on the ocean floor. The interior color of the shell can range from pale uniform pinks, greens, and reds to swirling grained patterns in several hues. The "heart" area where the animal attaches itself to the shell looks like a multi-colored burl.

There are about 200 types of abalone. Nine grow off the coast of California, but only four of these are cut commercially for inlay sheets. Black and red abalone are distinguishable by the "bark" on the outside of the shell, green and pink abalone by the inside color. When crushed to a powder, the color of the bark changes to a much lighter hue, but it is fairly useless for inlay purposes because the texture of this portion of the shell is unpredictable and doesn't lend itself easily to uniform slabbing. Occasionally a piece can be cut into the desired shape without crumbling into flakes, if a thin nacreous backing is left beneath the bark to give it more support.

The largest of these four commercially cut shells is red abalone. Record size for this type is about 12½" across, although 10" is considered trophy sized. Most shell used for inlay runs 7" to 9½", which means larger flat pieces can be slabbed from red abalones than from other types. Frequently, parasitic worm holes, stress cracks, or disease will limit the yield from these shells.

Green abalone is smaller and more curved than red, and the slab size is correspondingly smaller. The intense colors found on the inside of this shell make it more desirable and thus more expensive. "Rippled" abalone, which has an undulating wavy pattern to it, comes from the outer edge of the green shell as well.

Black abalone is my personal favorite, as the heart area has a depth and pearlescent quality that closely resembles blue-green opal.

The most beautiful of the abalones comes from New Zealand and is called paua (pronounced "pow-a"). Its coloring is predominantly electric blue with flashes of green and rose throughout. Paua is small and thin shelled, and many of the shells are worm-ridden. Exports from New Zealand are tightly controlled, so this abalone is not readily available in commercial quantities, but you can buy whole shells from lapidary suppliers and cut pieces yourself.*

Mother-of-pearl is a bivalve with two shells facing each other completely enclosing the critter inside. It can grow to a foot or more at the widest expanse and is somewhat mitten-shaped, with the "thumb" being near the hinged section. For some reason the "right-hand" section is always on the ocean floor and grows thicker and flatter than the upper half. From this lower shell, near the hinge, is where pearl knife handles and pistol grips are usually cut. Mother-of-pearl is a creamy iridescent white, and some pieces reveal pink and green flashes when moved around under a light source. The nacre closest to the bark is frequently a vibrant rippling gold color in animals harvested from the Philippines. These pieces are available at a slightly higher cost than regular mother-of-pearl.

Black mother-of-pearl grows around Tahiti and is finally readily available in plates again after 10 or more years of inaccessibility. The colors range from a smoky iridescent black to purple and brown with lots of streaks and ripply effects.

* Pink abalone used to be slabbed commercially, but it has some serious drawbacks that relegate it to a "shell of last resort." It isn't very large or common, and when cut into pieces, it tends to flake apart easily. The nacre is similar to green abalone, but the problems involved in cutting usable pieces are formidable.

Flashes of red and green appear here and there, and the color gradually gives way to white mother-of-pearl as the thin black layer is sanded away.

Before describing other materials, I have to stress that while the dust from cutting or sanding these shells is not toxic in and of itself (it's mainly calcium carbonate), the particles are sharp-edged and abrasive; if inhaled often enough, they can irritate the interior lining of your lungs, which build up a layer of mucosal covering around the pieces of dust, making breathing difficult. I've been told that this dust stays in permanently, so use a vacuum when you cut this stuff. I'll show you how mine is hooked up in the section on tools.

Metals are a bit easier to deal with than shell, at least during the cutting stage. Abalone hardness is about $2\frac{1}{2}$ to $3\frac{1}{2}$ on the Mohs' scale, and mother-of pearl is 3–4, but both vary in density and grain sometimes when least expected, causing the saw to zip out someplace it's not wanted. In contrast, the metals are uniform in density and fairly easy to cut. I usually buy silver and gold in 18–20 gauge sheets cut to the size I need for the project at hand. I get copper, brass, aluminum, and Dixgold (a brass alloy similar in color to 18k gold) by the square foot, since they're inexpensive. I also use silver and gold bezel and inlay it skinny side up for pieces requiring thin lines of metal.

Each type of wood has its own distinct peculiarities that you will become familiar with only through constant practice and experimentation. Sometimes I'll buy a pack of veneer samples to have a wide selec-

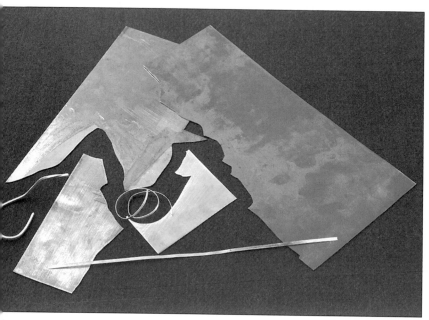

▼ Sheet metals and bezel.

tion on hand, as well as pressure-dyed veneers to get colors not available in natural wood. Scrap wood from friends who make furniture is also a good source. I resaw these pieces to about ⅛" thick for inlay use. They hold together better at that thickness and don't chip out as much when cut with the jeweler's saw.

A word of warning about veneers is in order here: veneers are normally sold in two thicknesses, ¼₈" and ¼₀", and the latter is becoming more common because of higher yield per log, but it is a major pain in the neck to inlay, especially during the final sanding. An intricately cut piece is no fun to replace if it's been sanded through during the last stages of a job, so whenever possible, go with the thicker stock. It's easier to take more material off than to put some back. Thin cut woods down to ¼₆" are available from West Friendship Hardwoods, listed in the Suppliers section.

Stones and gems are used sporadically in inlay work. Normally, when they are used, they will be inlaid after the other ma-

▲ Wood veneers.

terials. In order to keep them from falling apart, stone slabs have to be cut thicker than the shell or wood, and therefore must be inlaid deeper to minimize or eliminate sanding afterward. I've had some stone pieces cut by a lapidary, because they were too hard to cut with a jeweler's saw, but it is possible to find samples with hardness less than 3 that are usable, soapstone being one of them.

Faceted gems used for highlights are glued in after the finish is buffed and holes are countersunk, so the girdle of the stone fits flush with the finished surface. This practice allows the gem to flash and refract light at different angles.

Here we are at the politically sensitive part of the materials section: bone, antler, ivory, and vegetable ivory (tagua nut). I'll just give a brief description of each, and you can decide whether to include it in your palette or not. I do recommend, however, that when you are doing an inlay for someone else, you first find out that person's views on these materials before you build something that may be refused or thrown at you.

I use bone and antler occasionally in my work, but am not really enthusiastic about their qualities as inlay materials. Both are somewhat porous in the outer layers. If they're buffed to a gloss finish, the buffing compound can be difficult to remove, leaving a speckled, dirty look to the piece. In the center of antlers is a highly webbed area that is extremely porous. I sometimes use portions of this area for pieces needing a certain visual texture.

There are seven types of ivory: hippo tusk, elephant, fossil mastodon, boar, narwhale, whale teeth, and walrus. Hippo tusks have a very hard layer of enamel on the outside that must be ground off before cutting, but, once inside, the material (ba-

▶ Ivory.

♣ THE ART of INLAY

sically calcium phosphate) is very white with no grain or growth-layer markings. It's relatively soft and easy to work with.

Most of these ivories have a Mohs' hardness between 2 and 2.75. Elephant ivory is usually a creamy white color but can vary from gray to green or blond yellow, depending on the country it came from. When cut in sections across the tusk, it has a peculiar grain pattern resembling intersecting concentric circles. Cut with the length of the tusk, elephant ivory has long, closely spaced parallel growth lines.

Walrus tusk is smaller in diameter and length than elephant, and the interior is similar in appearance to tapioca pudding or closely packed bubbles, more finely grained in female tusks than in male ones.

Whale teeth, which come from either killer or sperm whales, are white, with no obvious grain.

Of the above types of ivory, the only kind that is still available in the United States is elephant ivory that was imported before 1976 to certain licensed dealers. If you buy some, you must keep the paperwork, which will have government stamps on it.

Tortoise shell has a somewhat similar status. It can no longer be imported, but if someone has one in the country already, it can be sold and used. If you have access to a tortoise shell, it would still be advisable to check with your state's Fish and Game Department before using it, as the laws may vary from state to state.

A perfectly acceptable source of ivory is fossilized mammoth (or mastodon) ivory, which is 30,000 years old. The grain configuration resembles elephant ivory, and its colors range from cream to tan, brown, or black. Tusks usually have cracks due to shrinkage that have to be worked around, but there is plenty of fossilized ivory, and no animals are being pushed to the brink of extinction to supply it.

The last source of "ivory" is tagua nut from Central America. These nuts are actually 2"-long palm seeds that grow in a fruit the size of a human head. They are about 98 percent cellulose and are similar in workability and color to ivory. Close examination by an expert will reveal the difference, and the size can be limiting for some projects, but it's a nice substitute and readily available. Many lapidary and jeweler suppliers have tagua nuts in stock.

▶ Tagua nut.

Tools

O NE OF THE ADVANTAGES of starting out in the world of inlay is the relatively low cost of the tools needed. If you already work with wood or jewelry, you probably have a head start in this area. The space required is minimal as well; a single bench or desk is enough.

Following is a description of the basic tools necessary to do a complete inlay.

1. A jeweler's saw frame is an adjustable frame with a wooden handle and screw clamps at the top and bottom to hold the jeweler's blades firmly. I normally use 3/0 blades for cutting everything, but sizes range from 8/0 (the tiniest) on up through 0, 1, 2, 3, etc., for heavy, coarse work, depending on your particular needs. Jeweler's blades are sold in packs of a dozen. The 3/0 blades I use cost around $2.20 per pack. If you break a blade, just throw it away and put a new one in, as shortening the saw frame to fit the remaining piece takes more time than it's worth. The saw frame pictured here can handle large pieces of material up to 6" across. Beginners may want to buy a 4" or 3" frame, as these are easier to wield.

2. A bench pin, V-block, or "bird's beak" is a wooden plank with a V-shaped slot cut into it that extends straight out from the workbench. The shell or other material is placed on the surface of the block when cutting the shape with the jeweler's saw. My block has a vacuum attachment above and below it to suck dust away while I'm cutting. The block is also

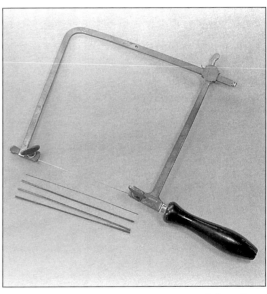

▲ Jeweler's saw frame with blades.

▲ V-block
with a vacuum attachment.

tapered to the front edge from underneath, so I can pinch small pieces between my fingers and slide them off, to prevent them from being sucked into the vacuum.

3. A good cannister vacuum is a must, not only for the abrasive shell dust, but because some wood dust can be quite obnoxious, and a vacuum also keeps dust from obscuring the top of the drawing as you cut through it. My vacuum is situated outside my shop with the hose running through the shop wall. This configuration reduces the noise level considerably, as well as eliminating any residual dust that makes it through the filter. Some inlayers like to place a fine mesh screen over the end of the vacuum tube to eliminate the need for searching the bag for lost pieces, but I usually let the machine take larger cast-off chunks of material and, therefore, don't screen mine.

4. A set of needle files is handy, especially to clean up ragged cuts on things like lettering, which need to have perfectly smooth edges. Medium (#2) files are adequate for this purpose. Some slightly larger rattail and flat mill files will also be useful.

5. One tool I've found to be of inestimable value over the years is a pair of vise-grip sheet metal pliers. This is a spring-loaded plierlike clamp that has long flat jaws for clamping lengthy pieces of any material. I've shortened the jaws to just under an inch across and use the pliers to grip small pieces while I file them smooth. I previously used regular pliers or glass-cutter's pliers, because they are manufactured for parallel jaw action, but they gave my hand cramps and often crushed the shell I

▼ Vise-grips.

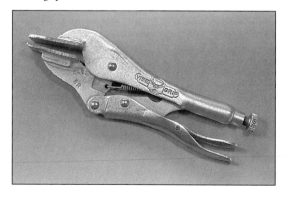

was trying to hold. The spring-loaded pliers can be adjusted to different pressures to accurately hold the material, which makes filing much easier.

6. Other clamps that will come in handy are large and small spring-loaded types and possibly some deep-throated wooden cam-operated ones. A useful clamping device that I have in my shop is called a "go-deck," or "go-bar." It originated in the Orient and is now used by many instrument makers as well. The go-deck consists of four threaded rods fixed in a bench surface with a sturdy top-plate that is adjustable for height, via nuts and washers. The two pieces to be glued together are placed on the bench under the top-plate and wooden dowels are fixed between the top-plate and the upper piece of the two to be glued. The top-plate is adjusted beforehand so the dowels will be bent when in place. This process offers a consistent clamping pressure over small or large areas, whether or not the surfaces are uneven. I use this method to glue large inlay plates into the surface of domed banjo resonators, with great results. A less elegant, but service-able solution would be to place wax paper on top of the freshly glued-in inlay and heap sand bags on top of that.

7. A miniature router for digging out the inlay cavity will probably represent your greatest single expense. I'm currently using a flex-shaft Dremel tool, not because I'm particularly fond of it, but because it was given to me and still works. The Foredom Company also makes a flex-shaft unit. Other small handheld routers costing around $100 will take different-sized collets for gripping various tool shank diameters. Whatever you end up with, make certain it will hold bit shafts down to $\frac{1}{16}$". I use carbide dental burrs for finishing up routing around edges of cuts and $\frac{1}{8}$" shank router bits for digging out large interior areas. A flat router base that is adjustable for bit depth is also necessary. If you choose a flex-shaft router, you'll probably have to make one of these yourself. The handheld Dremel models have an optional router base, but the flat plastic plate on the bottom usually isn't quite flat, so build one out of $\frac{1}{8}$" Plexiglas or aluminum as a substitute.

▲ "Go-deck."

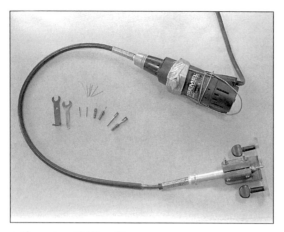

▲ The router with bits and base.

If you really want to get fancy, several companies make air-operated hand pieces that reach over 100,000 RPM. These can be costly, some being around $800, and they also need an adequate air compressor to run them.

8. The correct adhesive can make the difference between a really nice piece of art that will last and one that causes you extra hours of work before you consider it acceptable.

When there are many pieces in one inlay, I glue them together into one unit before inlaying them into the surface of the wood. This is done one piece at a time as they're cut, by placing them on a thin flexible metal scraper and using the cyanoacrylate (superglue) type of adhesive to fix them in their correct relative positions. After they dry they can be popped off of the flexible metal.

I also use the cyanoacrylates for gluing most inlays into the cavities in which they finally rest. These glues are favored for several reasons: they are quick setting, dry without bubbling as much as epoxies, and are clear, so they tend to take on the colors of whatever material they are inlaid into, especially the darker ones. Cyanoacrylates also have fairly low viscosity, so they will seep into areas that thicker glues can't easily reach.

For large inlaid plates, like the backs of banjo resonators, I use 24-hour epoxies, which give me more time to adjust the clamps before they set up. I stay away from aliphatic resins and other wood glues because they don't adhere to metals and some other materials as well as I'd like.

Be sure your workspace is adequately ventilated when using all types of glues and epoxies; this is especially important when working with cyanoacrylates as the fumes can be quite nasty, causing watering eyes, stuffy nose, or more severe allergic reactions.

Drawings

A GOOD DRAWING IS THE ESSENCE of a tastefully executed inlay. Mistakes made during the succeeding steps may be covered up without being noticeable, but a job perfectly executed from a poorly designed drawing will be a piece that looks like someone wasted his or her time.

For those of you who are mechanically adept but cower in terror at the thought of drawing an acceptable design on a blank piece of paper, fear not. I am also unable to compose a drawing entirely from my mind. The trick is to do it in stages so you eventually sneak up on a finished product you can be proud of.

One of the technological luxuries I am indebted to is the modern copy machine. If I see something I like in a book, I'll make a copy of it to trace over, rather than tracing it directly from the book. Tracing from a book not only leaves ugly indentations around the traced object from the weight of the pencil (librarians will hate you for this), but even with the sheerest of tracing paper it's difficult to trace the detail on a photograph. When copying photos from a book, set the copier on the lightest setting. Then place the resulting copy on a glass sheet with a light source shining through from behind. You can even do this by taping the copy and the tracing paper to a window. Then trace the major outlines and as much detail as possible with a sharp *hard* pencil lead. I use a drafting pencil with 8H lead, sharpening it every few strokes. At this point it's not critical to have very fine lines, but on the final drawing it is.

When the tracing is done, remove it from the original, put the original aside, and trace over the tracing. You'll be amazed at how much you can clean up the first tracing. Make the lines as clean and fine as possible this time. Remember, an inlay is basically a puzzle whose pieces you have to cut yourself, so be sure that the

▲ Tracing with just the outlines of the pieces, and tracing with all the detail.

lines for each separate piece meet another line, enclosing a specific area. If you draw detail lines to be engraved afterward, they don't have to meet any perimeter lines, but where pieces are adjacent to others, an incomplete outline means trouble.

When you have your final tracing, make eight to ten copies of it, and you'll be ready for the next step. If you need to enlarge your drawing, find a copier that will shrink or enlarge in increments of 1 percent. These copiers are easier to set to the exact size you need than the ones which only have two or three preset sizes. An enlarged copy of your tracing will make the lines thicker, so trace the enlargement and makes copies of the tracing. The reason for this will become evident when we get into the section on cutting.

For drawings with extreme amounts of engraving detail, I recommend one final tracing with all the detail, and another tracing with just the outlines of the pieces. (See the two versions of the dragon inlay design as an example.) This will help prevent confusion during the cutting process.

Once you've cut some simple inlays to get the general idea, you might feel frisky enough to try a more complex theme. Again, you're faced with the drawing dilemma. I'll use a concrete example of how I deal with this.

The drawing at right is for an inlay I did on the back of a banjo resonator. The circle is 10" in diameter. My greatest ally here was my library card. At the library I collected books on riverboats, Currier and Ives prints, 19th century fashion, illustrated Mark Twain editions, famous outlaws, buffalo hunters, and whatever else seemed relevant. I made copies of everything that looked remotely usable, in various enlarged and shrunk percentages, keeping in mind the size the finished piece would be.

For the riverboat I did the original tracings larger than the finished product so I could get in as much detail as possible, then shrank them to appropriate sizes. When I had final tracings of everything in the sizes I wanted, I arranged and rearranged them within the bounds of a 10" circle, until I felt the composition was right.

Composition is something I cannot teach. My only advice would be that if you feel comfortable with the final compilation, go for it, and in the meantime read as much

▼ Drawing for riverboat resonator.

about art appreciation, perspective, anatomy, and composition as you can stomach.

When I was satisfied with the arrangement, I put a large sheet of tracing paper over the whole collection of other tracings and did a final drawing, which I later made a dozen copies of. After the main elements were in place, it was easier to draw freehand the dock and the mountains on the other side of the river.

Something I should warn you about is using copyrighted drawings to make your inlays. If your inlay is for yourself, there will probably be no problem, but if you're planning to sell it or have a photo of it in a magazine, you need permission from the artist, and may have to pay a design fee as well. Some artists are testier about this than others.

Even if you alter the original artwork to some extent, the change may not void the copyright status. Changing the medium, i.e., making an inlay instead of a painting, may help, but don't wait until you get taken to court to find out for sure. The best rule is to either produce original work or get permission from the artist.

Another alternative is to use the wealth of copyright-free design books available. Dover publishes so many of these books covering all styles that they could keep you busy inlaying for a lifetime without having to draw at all.

▶ Design books to draw from.

COLOR GALLERY TWO:

INLAY PORTFOLIO

SELECTED NORTH AMERICAN INLAY ARTISTS

◄ "Tropical Dream" wood sculpture by Faren Dancer, artist from Santa Fe, New Mexico. One of the unusual aspects of Faren's work is the three-dimensional layered look. In this piece, the sky is made from lapis lazuli with red abalone clouds and gold sun. The palm trees are malachite and zebrawood, chestnut, and/or obechi wood. The water is turquoise; the bamboo is green abalone and silver. The birds are various types of shell, with gold feet and beaks.
PHOTOGRAPHER: FAREN DANCER.

▲ ► ► A peghead, neck, and resonator by Renee Karnes, banjo builder from Rescue, California, inlaid in a symmetric floral motif. Various shells, wood, and metals, with nice touches of engraving.
PHOTOGRAPHER: RENEE KARNES.

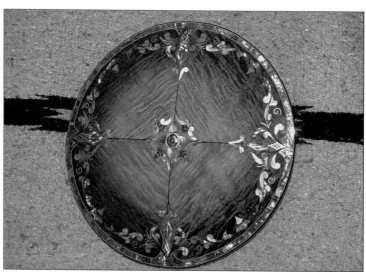

❧ THE ART of INLAY

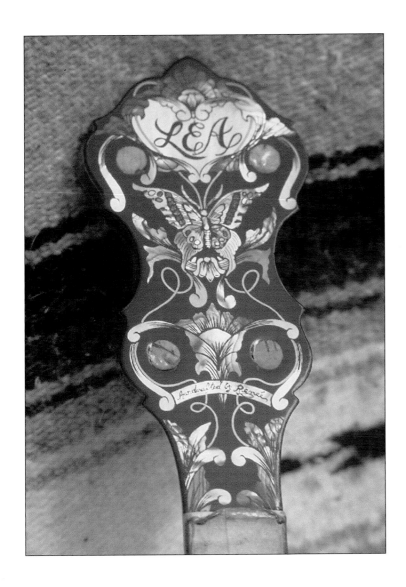

▲ ▶ ▶ Grit Laskin, one of the most astonishing inlay artists in North America,
frequently uses live models and photography while composing a theme.
His self-portrait and snow leopard are exercises in restraint
but fully detailed and beautifully engraved.
PHOTOGRAPHER: BRIAN PICKELL.

❦ THE ART of INLAY

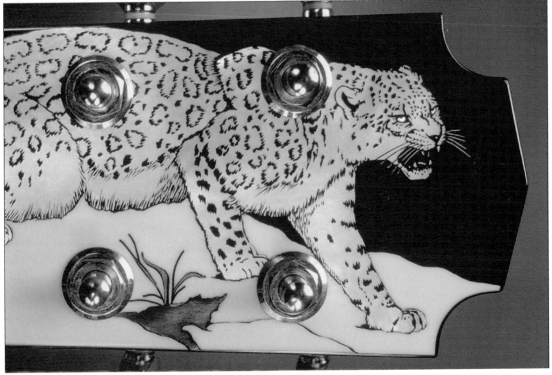

▼ Grit Laskin uses the fingerboard and peghead as a window to a larger world. You can almost see the rest of the geese in this flock flying past.
PHOTOGRAPHER: BRIAN PICKELL.

▼ "Unravelling Man," by Grit Laskin, drawn at the customer's request, loosely follows Escher's "Unravelling Head." Materials include ivory, silver, copper, abalone, maple, mother-of-pearl, and gold mother-of-pearl.
PHOTOGRAPHER: BRIAN PICKELL.

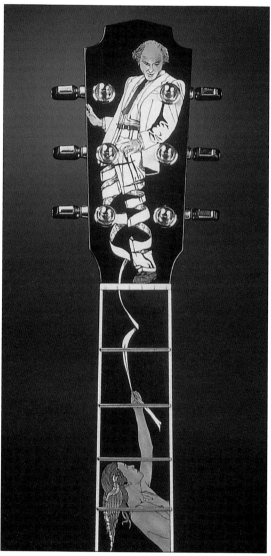

♣ THE ART of INLAY

◄ Close-up of "Tropical Dream" wood sculpture by Faren Dancer, artist from Santa Fe, New Mexico.
PHOTOGRAPHER: FAREN DANCER.

◄ ▼ ► Ren Ferguson's inlay work has had a lot of exposure from his work on Gibson acoustic guitars.
Note the raised gems in the crown inlay (bottom, next page), and the use of various materials in his vines, which gives them more visual interest. The design on the guitar at left is a cross between Art Nouveau and Arabic styles.
PHOTOGRAPHER: REN FERGUSON.

▲ Richard Hoover's vine, edge purfling,
and bridge inlay give this Santa Cruz guitar
a very elegant look. The inlay adds to the beauty of the
instrument without being overbearing.
PHOTOGRAPHER: PAUL SCHRAUB.

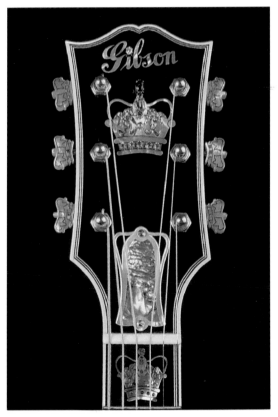

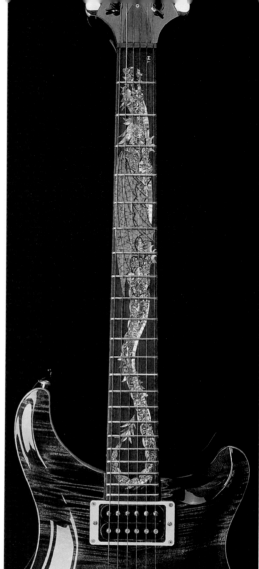

▲ Dragons for Paul Reed Smith by Larry Sifel of Pearl Works. Larry turned out 52 of these on his CAD-CAM setup. The dragons consist of 201 pieces of abalone, mother-of-pearl, coral, and turquoise. One of these instruments is the first electric guitar to be displayed at the Smithsonian Institute.
PHOTOGRAPHER: DENNIS VOSS.

◄ Inlay by Doug Irwin, instrument by Larry Robinson. The inlay is made from silver sheet and square silver stock, with various pieces of abalone and mother-of-pearl. A nice Art Nouveau look.
PHOTOGRAPHER: RICHARD LLOYD.

♣ THE ART of INLAY

◄ Linda Manzer's "Endangered Species" guitar is built from sustainable yield hardwoods, and the inlays represent endangered or extinct Canadian wildlife. PHOTOGRAPHER: BRIAN PICKELL.

▼ Manzer's "Moon Walk" peghead graces one of her handmade guitars. Materials include maple, purple hearts, mother-of-pearl, and ivory from old piano keys. PHOTOGRAPHER: LINDA MANZER.

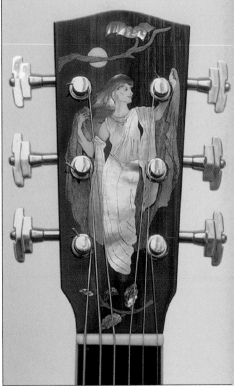

▲ ▶ ▶ The Grove Long-Neck Banjosaurus,
made for George Grove of the Kingston Trio.
The fingerboard inlay took about 400 hours.
Materials were turquoise, coral, cactus,
black pearl, gold pearl, white pearl, abalone shell,
various kinds of rock, rosewood, and ebony.
By Greg Deering, Jeremiah Deering, and Charles Nietzel
of the Deering Banjo Company.
PHOTOGRAPHER: PETER FIGEN.

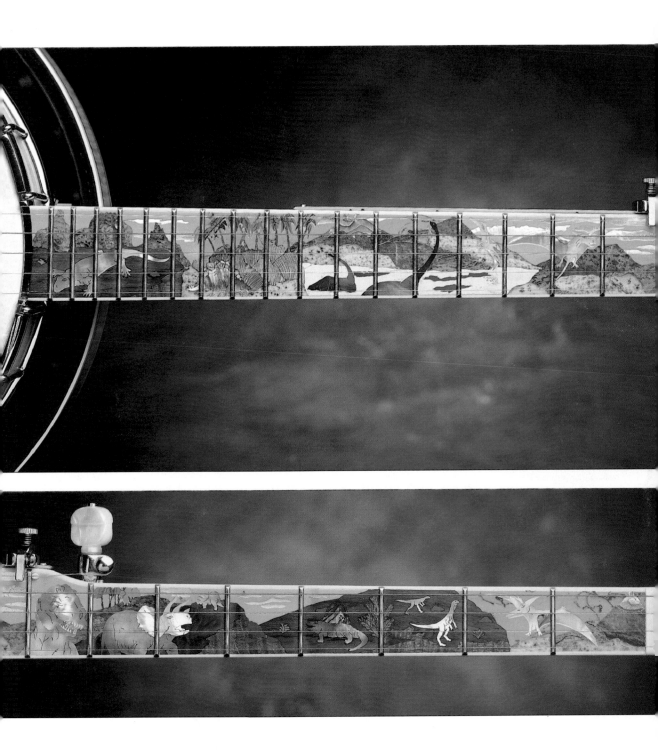

◀ Rick Turner inlay and instrument conversion.
Rick says this bass started out as a Guild "Bluesbird" in 1968.
He put a carved archtop and back on it and inlaid some
"psychedelic madness" on the fingerboard for Phil Lesh
of the Grateful Dead. It was updated in 1993 with nylon strings
and piezoelectric pickups.
PHOTOGRAPHER: RICK TURNER.

▼ Steve Klein is known in the luthier world as an innovative
designer, and this quality shows in his inlay work. The top of
this guitar is inlaid with paper-thin strips of rosewood, and the
soundhole rosette of ebony and abalone heart is removable.

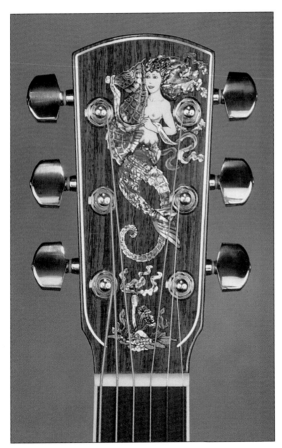

◄ ▼ The Larriveé Guitar Co. has several new inlay styles for each year's production. For the most part, these beautiful designs are produced by machine, then hand-engraved after leveling. The owl and the deer peghead inlay, a custom design for Joan Baez, uses just a few pieces and was exquisitely engraved by Wendy Larriveé.
PHOTOGRAPHERS: RON HIPP & FRED DUSEL.

▶ ▲ ▶ Michael Kemnitzer (Nugget Mandolins).
One reason that these inlays are so attractive
is Kemnitzer's choice of grain patterns in the shell he used.
Note the circular pattern in the abalone halo
over the goddess's head. The abalone purfling
around the body scroll in the mandolin
was beautifully executed as well.
PHOTOGRAPHER: JIM RANTALA.

Getting Started

Now it's time to pull out your stash of inlay materials and choose what will look best for each piece. At this time you will use your artistic sensibilities to choose the grain pattern, direction, color, or texture to complement your overall design. Keep in mind where the inlay will finally rest when choosing materials. For instance, on the edge of a box that will be handled frequently, you might want to use silver instead of a veneer, because the metal will stand up to a certain amount of abuse better than the wood. If the inlay is to be in a musical instrument fingerboard, consider the wear and tear of strings grinding on it and choose accordingly. Also remember that woods and most metals, with the notable exceptions of gold and platinum, will tarnish over time if left unsealed. Even under a laquered surface many materials will change color somewhat.

The reason you have made multiple copies of your final drawing is that you will be cutting around the outside of each separate piece (using an X-ACTO knife or razor blade) and rendering adjacent pieces of the copy unusable. Take a fresh copy each time you cut out a new piece. The more complex the drawing is, the more copies you will need. You should keep a master copy and perhaps number or letter each piece as you go, especially if many of them are of similar shape or size. Be careful not to curl up the edges of the paper pieces as they're cut from the copy. They glue down much better if they remain flat.

Go ahead and glue the paper onto the mate-

▼ X-ACTO knife with copy pieces.

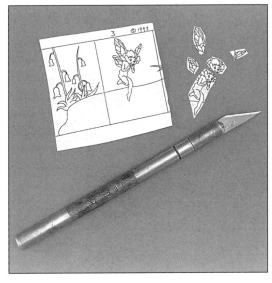

rials you've chosen. I use cyanoacrylate for this step, too, because it holds together well enough when you saw out the shapes but can still be peeled off afterward. To avoid gluing your fingers together, put a little glue on the shell (or whatever material you're working with) and stab the paper with the X-ACTO knife. You should be able to lift the paper this way and place it onto the glue. Then tamp down the edges with the knife point.

If you've chosen a veneer to glue part of your drawing on, coat the veneer's reverse side with a thin layer of cyanoacrylate, using a razor blade or stick to spread it around. This layer will help to stabilize the piece, as cutting through veneers without this backing tends to rip large chips out.

Don't underestimate the importance of a well-ventilated workplace when working with any of the glues.

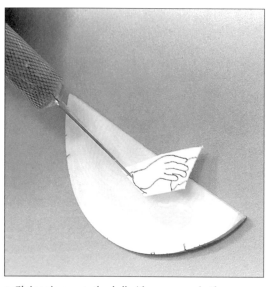

▲ Gluing pieces onto the shell with an X-ACTO knife.

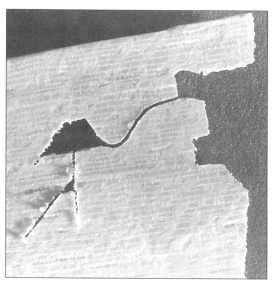

▲ Veneer, backed and unbacked.

Optical Tricks

OF ALL THE MATERIALS SUITABLE for inlay purposes, shell is the one I enjoy working with the most. As shell is held near a single light source, the colors will become brilliant or dull as the blank is twisted around or wiggled. Many people who try inlay overlook this property when laying out their designs. They will spend inordinate amounts of time matching wood grain on guitar or banjo bodies, but then they glue designs on shell blanks to take advantage of the space on the blank, not thinking of the effects of light refraction.

A few examples of shell's possibilities should give you enough ideas to get excited and perhaps develop your own techniques that haven't been thought of before. For instance, an inlay that travels the length of a guitar fingerboard can be set up to "flash on" entirely from one vantage point, or one section at a time, all the way up the neck. Chuck Erikson sets his shell blanks in a shallow tub of water next to a single light source with the inlay drawing on the bench next to it. Having the shell under water makes it easier to decide how to orient the individual pieces to take advantage of these qualities before gluing the sections of drawing to them.

Another method, used especially to ensure continuity of long stretches of abalone (such as purfling strips around guitar tops or other borders), is to match the butt ends of the shell strips to each other. With this technique, the heart area of one piece faces the heart area of the next and long grain matches with long grain, pale to pale, etc. This way, the eye isn't distracted by obvious joint lines in the border.

You should also experiment with the natural grain lines and shapes inherent in the shell blanks themselves. This may necessitate making your drawing conform to the shell, rather than the other way around, but the results can be spectacular. I have two abalone pieces that were split from one blank so they fold out like a book (strangely enough, these are known as book-matched slabs) and look exactly like some weird dragon's head, face on. I've had them for years and am waiting for the right opportunity to draw an entire design around these two pieces.

"Bull's-eyes" are airholes that have grown over with more shell and can be used for halos or eyes; long striped pieces can be rainbows, among other things. Chuck Erikson has used horizontally striped abalone for the center of a candle flame, with gold mother-of-pearl for the outside, which makes the candle appear to flicker as the piece is moved around. He has also done the sun's corona out of gold mother-of-pearl, and the body of the sun out of black pearl, orienting the refractions opposite each other so that any movement makes the orb appear to pulse. Another example of the inherent light qualities of shell may be seen on page 31, showing two views of the same inlay of zebras.

Combining all these techniques with the refractive choices requires more shell inventory than just slapping things together, but leaves a much more satisfying impression when the final product is viewed. Your imagination is the only limit to creativity here.

Cutting

THE CUTTING STAGE of the inlay process is the most demanding physically and mentally, although, as your technique improves with practice, it becomes quite enjoyable and even meditative to a degree. It will be much easier to begin cutting the pieces if you are in a comfortable position and can see what you are doing clearly.

I'm using a comfy adjustable swivel office chair with rollers on the bottom. The rollaway aspect is handy but not absolutely necessary. The seat is 21½" off the floor so that my feet can rest flat on the floor when I'm sitting down. Clamped to the bench, my V-block is 38" off the floor, just about mid-chest level when I sit, and when I bend my head down to see what I'm doing, my eyes are about 8" above the block.

I wear a pair of reading glasses to avoid eyestrain at that distance. It's important not to squint your eyes when cutting. I've been asked many times if I wear jeweler's magnifying headpieces and the answer is an emphatic *"no!"* The reason I don't like them is that they have such a short focal length that if I move my head even the slightest bit the image blurs, which gives me headaches, ultimately hindering rather than improving accurate cutting. It's been my experience that I'm better off with vision as close to normal as possible. After all, that's how the finished product will be viewed. There are low-power magnifiers available that have a longer focal length, but my reading glasses accomplish essentially the same thing.

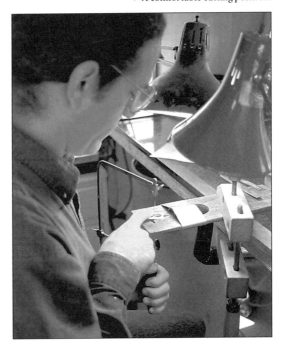

▼ A comfortable cutting position.

It's important to have plenty of light on both sides of your saw while cutting so shadows from the sawblade don't obscure the lines of the drawing. I use two adjustable hooded lamps with a 100-watt bulb in each. These are situated close to the block on either side, low enough not to shine in my eyes, but high enough so the saw doesn't smash into them on the up-stroke. Other inlay artists use fluorescent/incandescent combination lights and won't cut shell without them.

Even though I know a few people who grind shell and cut inlays without using a mask or vacuum, I'd like to have a normal lifespan, so I don't follow their example. The vacuum I use is extremely powerful and is hooked up so that it pulls dust from above and below the block. I can't see any dust particles floating away in the hot air from the lamps, so I don't wear a mask, but it's a good idea to use one as an added safety precaution.

Before you go to the next step, here is a simple design for you to try the cutting techniques on. It is composed of three separate pieces but will give you a solid idea of what is involved in cutting inside and outside corners, straight lines and curves. You will also understand the necessity of just barely cutting the lines away to make one piece fit snugly into another. Before you decide that it looks too easy, check it out first. I will also tell you that my girlfriend's seven-year-old daughter has cut this shape, and everything fit together when she was done.

Once your setup is complete, you're ready to cut your first piece. Fit the jeweler's saw (handle end down) with a blade, teeth facing forward and pointing down, with enough tension on the blade so you can push it in maybe a sixteenth of an inch at the center. If it's too loose, you won't be able to guide it along the cutting line, and if it's too tight, it'll probably snap on the first stroke. You should be able to pluck the blade and hear a nice, high-pitched *ping* if it's adjusted to the correct tension.

Take the saw in your dominant hand (I'm a lefty, but use whichever hand affords you the most control) and hold it so the blade is straight up and down. This position is the hardest thing for beginners to get a sense of: how to hold the saw truly per-

▲ Sample design.

♣ THE ART *of* INLAY

pendicular to the shell while paying attention to cutting the outline accurately. Maintaining this position has a lot to do with keeping your wrist relaxed. Your fingers should curl around the saw handle, but not too tightly. When tracking around curves you can roll the handle by moving your fingers back and forth. The resulting cut will be smoother than if you turn your whole hand from the wrist.

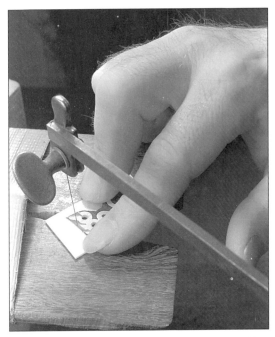

▲ Index finger position.

Hold down the piece you're cutting on the "V"-block with the end hanging over the open "V" section a bit. Use two fingers to clamp it tightly, one on either side of the "V", and maneuver it around as you cut. Begin the cut with steady strokes directly into the piece and try to keep the blade near the edge of the V slot whenever possible. You don't have to push the saw forward much. Let the weight of the stroke do the work for you. The main functions of your sawing hand are stroking straight up and down and turning corners. As your proficiency improves, you'll get to the point where you can turn the piece and the saw simultaneously.

The challenge at this stage is to maintain the pressure on the piece with one hand while keeping the saw hand relaxed. If you let up on the clamping pressure while sawing, the blade can snap, the piece may end up in the vacuum, or you could cut your finger.

Make some practice cuts before you begin your inlay. Try some straight cuts and see if you can stay right on the line. Then experiment with some curves.

When you need to cut around a sharp exterior corner, make the cut extend a little farther than the line, and *keeping the saw stroking*, turn the saw or the piece (or both) to the new saw direction. Don't try to move the saw forward during the turn. This process is somewhat akin to marching in place.

When turning the saw around in an interior angle, cut right

up to the end of the corner and back the saw out a little bit. Then, while stroking in place, turn the saw so that the blade cuts away from the line and rotate it 180 degrees. Now you can back the saw into the vertex of the angle and start cutting up the other side.

Cutting a shape out of the interior of another piece is known as piercing. You drill a small hole in the scrap section and run the blade through it before clamping the lower end to the saw frame. Piercing can also be used for cutting extremely delicate pieces. Drill a small hole next to the piece to be cut, thread the blade through, and cut around the design. This method leaves a rigid intact border around the piece that offers more support than a blank cut through from the edge.

The saw blades are rectangular, and the width of the cut, or kerf, is smaller than the front to back dimension. This blade shape allows you to do all kinds of tricky things to clean up mistakes. The size of the kerf also makes it imperative that you cut right on the drawn line. The kerf will be wider than the line on the drawing if your pencil was kept sharp, and when cutting, the object is to just barely shave off the line from each piece. You will be slightly undercutting each piece, and, when the cutting is done perfectly, everything will fit together beautifully, leaving the least possible gap between pieces. If you overcut the sizes, when everything is assembled some pieces won't fit at all, and you will need to do a great deal of filing to make it work.

The reason I emphasize keeping the drawing lines as thin as possible will become apparent at this stage. If you have two pieces in a drawing that are separated by a thick line, and the line gets completely cut away from around each piece, a relatively large and ugly space will be your constant reminder of the importance of good drawings. However, if you make your original drawings oversized, when you reduce them the lines will be thin and crisp.

If you deviate outside the line when cutting, you can turn the saw within the cut, and while sawing up and down, move it sideways down the cut. The saw acts almost like a file in this position and can help get you back on the line. If you cut too far inside the line, discard the piece and cut another one.

Just placing the saw at the edge of the shell when you start a cut will probably ensure that the blade will slide down the edge of the blank at the first downstroke. When you want to start at an exact location on the shell, hold the saw so the back of the blade touches the inside of the **V** slot on the cutting block. Then push the shell over the edge of the **V** slot until it wedges the blade exactly where you want the cut to start. Now when you make a downstroke the blade will bite in right where you want it.

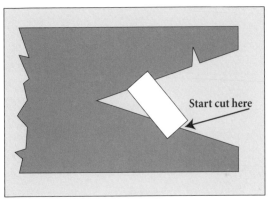

▲ Wedged cut.

Another way to help the blade go where you'd like it to is to place the index finger of your clamping hand directly behind the blade as you cut. The finger still clamps the piece on top of the block, while at the same time rolling in the direction of the cut, barely pushing the back of the blade. Cutting in this manner allows the saw hand to stroke and turn without pushing as well, giving you much more control over the process.

▼ Cutting around a circle.

Let's say you have to cut around a circle. Start with the wedge cut and saw into the shell as if you are going to cut directly across the diameter of the circle. Stop cutting when you reach the line and execute a 90 degree turn by stroking the saw in place and turning the blade at the same time. By the time you saw all the way around the circle and break through the end, there may be a little nub, which is easily filed off. If you try cutting the circle by gradually spiraling in from an outer orbit, you will not only waste a lot of time and shell, but the blade will likely pop out of the cut before you've completed your way around the circumference. You will also end

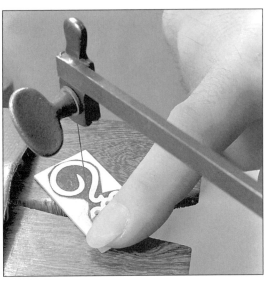

up having to file off more excess shell.

One sawing tip I'd like to share concerns your clamping hand. Use your first two fingers to clamp the shell down when starting a cut but switch to just the index finger immediately and hold it behind the blade, clamping the piece on the same side of the block as your saw arm. Having the saw cutting away from your finger is much more comforting than searching the vacuum for the portion you've cut off. Remember to keep pulling the piece back so the blade is always near the cutting block. This technique does take more strength than using two fingers to clamp with, however.

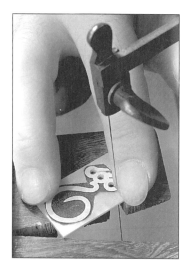

▲ Placing the index finger behind the blade

Another technique I've found helpful in accurate cutting is to glance a little bit ahead of where the blade is while continuing the saw stroke. Flick your eyes back and forth from where the blade is heading to where it is actually cutting the inlay material. It may sound strange, but I've found this method to be particularly useful in cutting long, straight lines.

Something you may have noticed in the photos of the cutting block is the miniature **V** slot cut at 90 degrees to the main slot. After years of losing tiny pieces to the maw of the vacuum, I finally came up with this solution. The slot is far enough away from the vacuum so the cut pieces won't just fly into it, but close enough so the dust disappears.

When you cut an extremely small piece, finish the cut in this sideways slot with the larger portion of the piece resting on the edge of the block closest to you and the saw cutting away or to the side. Before you make the last few strokes releasing the piece from the rest of the material, clamp down on the little bugger with your index finger, preferably with the nail.

▼ Cutting a tiny piece

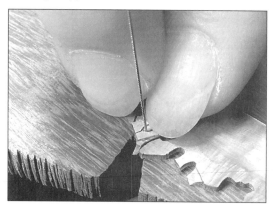

If you try to lift the entire excess portion off the inlay piece, you stand the chance of dropping the cut piece onto the floor or into the vacuum. While holding the piece in place with your finger, release the clamp on the lower end of the sawblade with the other hand. This technique takes some practice, but once you can do it, you will be able to slide the blade up and out of the shell and pull the whole shell, with the cut piece still enclosed within it, toward you. Pinching from under the block with your thumb, pull the shell off the end of the block and release the cut piece from between your thumb and forefinger and set it aside safely away from the vacuum. An on/off foot switch for the vacuum would be handy at this point, but not absolutely necessary.

If you are right-handed, your tendency will probably be to cut counterclockwise around exterior cuts and clockwise around interior cuts. This practice will afford you the best view of the side of the blade that is shaving off the line of the drawing. For us southpaws, it's just the opposite. As your cutting proficiency improves you'll find there will be times when it's advantageous to be able to cut interior and exterior lines from either direction. You may have to hover almost directly over the saw to accomplish this, but try it.

Filing pieces seems pretty straightforward, and it is. But if you want to steady both hands for greater accuracy, hold the cut piece with vise-grips and rest them on top of the cutting block. Holding the needle file with the other hand, rest part of the file shank on the outside edge of the block and push the inlay piece up to the file as you stroke. You'll find this holds the piece steadier than if you try to freehand it.

Here again, be aware of the necessity of filing perpendicular to the surface of the piece.

After you've cut some adjacent pieces, place them in position on a thin flexible steel scraper and pop a drop of superglue on them to hold them together. Inlaying one piece of material, even if the piece consists of many smaller pieces glued together, is infinitely easier than fumbling with a bunch of pieces in a glue-filled cavity.

If the design is really complex, make a reverse copy of the final tracing and glue each piece upside down on that copy. This method ensures that the inlay retains the intended shape, but it doesn't work as well if some of the cut pieces are of quite different thicknesses. Although the chosen grain and color of your material would be preserved by inlaying everything flush with the top of the pieces, routing the cavity to different depths to ensure a proper fit could prove to be a nightmare, especially if some pieces are quite a bit thicker than others. If all the pieces of the inlay are of similar thicknesses, this method will work well. You could glue everything together on top of a regular drawing, but before inlaying it you'd need to scrape all the paper off, since it would show through the spaces between pieces.

Any time you cut a large inlay with a great many pieces, the shape will begin to deviate from the drawing as you glue more pieces together. Small deviations in cutting add up, and the discrepancy will become magnified over large areas. The way I solve this problem is by gluing the pieces together in three or four separate sections, leaving the background pieces to be cut last. This works especially well when I'm doing something like the 10"-diameter banjo resonator inlays. As I cut the separate sections, I frequently lay the glued-up sections over the drawing so I can see how far off from the original it's getting to be.

When I reach the point where I have only the background pieces left to cut, I place all the finished sections where they belong on the drawing and slip the uncut background pieces between the drawing and the sections that are already cut. Then I clamp everything in place and use the X-ACTO knife to score new lines on the background sections. Using the new line as a guide, I then cut the background pieces and glue them to the finished sections. This procedure allows me to compensate for the inevitable deviations from the design that would otherwise result in an ill-fitting piece of work with visible gaps.

Advanced Techniques

A PLEASING INLAY STYLE I'VE USED many times on guitar and bass fingerboards is done with square silver stock. The photo seen on page 22 is of an electric bass fingerboard I designed and inlaid for John Paul Jones of the rock group Led Zeppelin.

I folded the drawing paper in half the long way and sketched the right side of the design, keeping in mind where the fingerboard position markers normally fall. When the sketch looked like it flowed from one area to the next, I flipped the tracing paper over and copied the right side to the left. I then bought ten feet of 12 gauge square silver wire.

The first time I attempted an inlay like this one I routed the cavity in the fingerboard and then bent the silver to fit the cavity. Big mistake. This resulted in an inlay that was obviously not symmetrical. A year or so later I tried it again on a 12-string guitar I was building, but this time I bent the silver for the left side of the drawing first. When that matched the drawing, I bent the right side silver to match the left side. I then glued the silver to the fingerboard and scribed around it in the manner I will describe later. You can see the difference fairly easily in the photo of both guitars on page 18.

An added attraction to the Jones fingerboard is the insertion of abalone pieces fitted exactly inside some of the enclosed areas of silver. With this construction method you can't expect the inlay to conform exactly to the original drawing, so inlay the silver first, and level it. Then trace the areas that need to be filled with shell and glue the tracings directly onto the abalone pieces. After cutting them out, rout the areas and glue the shell in. If you've traced accurately, you should have a nearly perfect fit.

Next, level and polish the shell and you're finished, unless

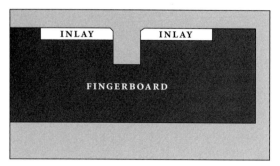

▲ Side view
of relieved inlay in fret slot

you're inlaying an instrument fingerboard. If so, cut through the sections where the inlay crosses the fret slots, and, using a small triangular file, relieve the slot sections where the inlay crosses from one to the next. This step makes the fretting and later refretting less likely to pull out inlaid sections.

Something else which is occasionally required of the inlayer is a person's signature. Signatures are not too difficult to do from metal sheet stock, but if mother-of-pearl or abalone is requested, the fragility of the piece during the cutting and scribing can be frustrating. Here is a method to help you cut these extremely thin lines without cracking any.

First, make half a dozen copies of the signature. Glue one copy onto the shell blank and one copy onto whatever type of wood the name will be inlaid into. Ebony is the best choice for this technique because you won't have to worry about matching the grain lines afterward.

Next, do any piercing cuts required, such as the insides of *o*'s or *b*'s. Accurate cutting is important during this step, so make sure the saw blade just touches the inside edge of the line.

Now cut the wooden pieces that fit into these holes and glue them in. When these pieces are dry, carefully cut around the outside lower half of the signature, leaving the upper half attached to the shell blank. Again, cut the corresponding piece from the wood blank and glue it to the outer edge of the signature. The wooden edge that doesn't sandwich up against the shell can be cut in any desired shape, but an irregular outline is harder to see after the whole plate has been inlaid.

The last cutting step is finishing the top half of the signature the same way as the bottom. You should now have an ebony plate with an irregular outline that completely encapsulates a fragile unbroken signature.

The steps to inlay it are the same as those described later.

One technique that shows up frequently on Korean inlay work gives the appearance of sun-baked clay, or *raku* pottery.

For lack of a better term, I'll call it the crackle finish. After the inlay pieces have been cut to shape, and the cavities have been cut to fit them into, glue the top surface of the shell to a sheet of paper. Make certain that all the shell surface is coated with the glue. When the glue is completely dry, tap the shell with a small hammer from the back until it is fractured to the texture you like. Then glue the pieces, still topped with paper, into the cavity and sand the paper off when the glue is dry. Experiment with some scrap pieces first, as some chunks tend to flake off with the hammer blows. They can be superglued back together if you can find the correct alignment.

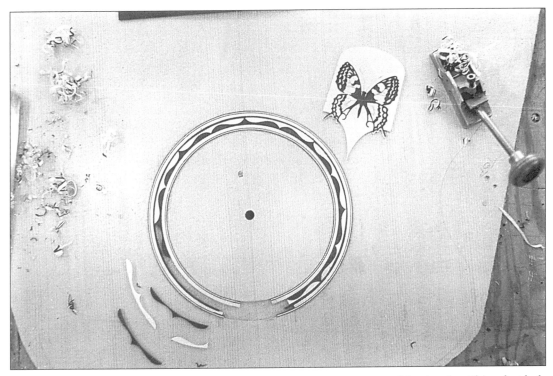

▲ Inlay pieces for a Klein walnut-body
guitar made for Joe Walsh.

INLAYS BY LARRY ROBINSON

▲ "Spider" banjo for Gibson Custom Shop, 1990. Web on resonator is aluminum dust glued into grooves. Spider has six emeralds for eyes. (ALL PHOTOS IN THIS SECTION ARE BY RICHARD LLOYD.)

▲ Centerpiece of Samurai triptych, 1993.
Twelve-and-a-half inches long with gilt base.
Inlay is in multiple materials, some of which
are tinted with colored inks after leveling.

▶ Banjo peghead featuring "spider" design
shown in closeup on previous page.

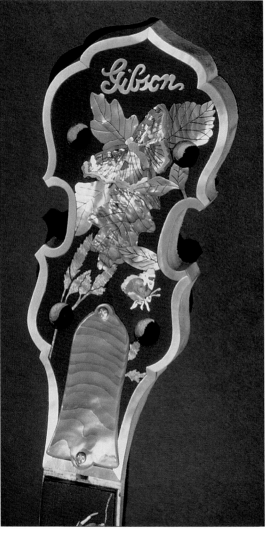

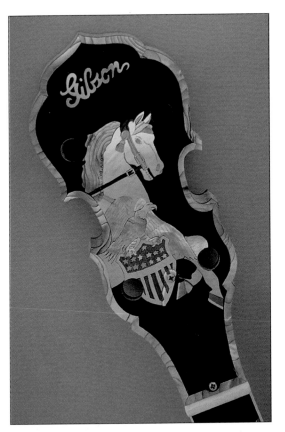

◄ ▼ ▼ "Carousel" banjo
for Gibson Custom Shop. Lots of tiny pieces and engraving.

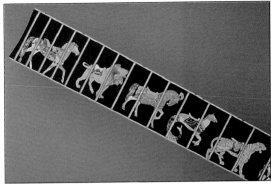

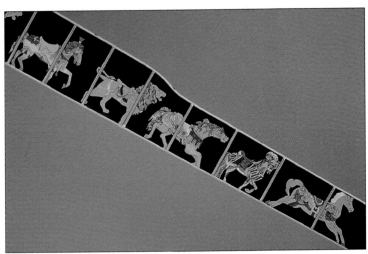

▲ ▶ "Venice" banjo for Gibson Custom Shop, 1991.
Resonator is mostly veneers, with some mother-of-pearl, and metal.
Renaissance vine down neck was easier than I thought it would be.

♣ THE ART of INLAY

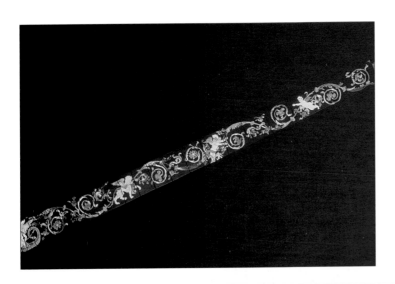

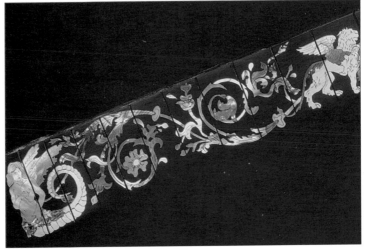

◄ "Signing of the Declaration" resonator, 1992, for Gibson. I've seen this inlay printed in several places, with no credit given to me for inlaying it.

▼ and ◄ (page 86, opposite).
Two riverboat resonators for the Tsumura collection, 1992 (below) and 1991, (left).

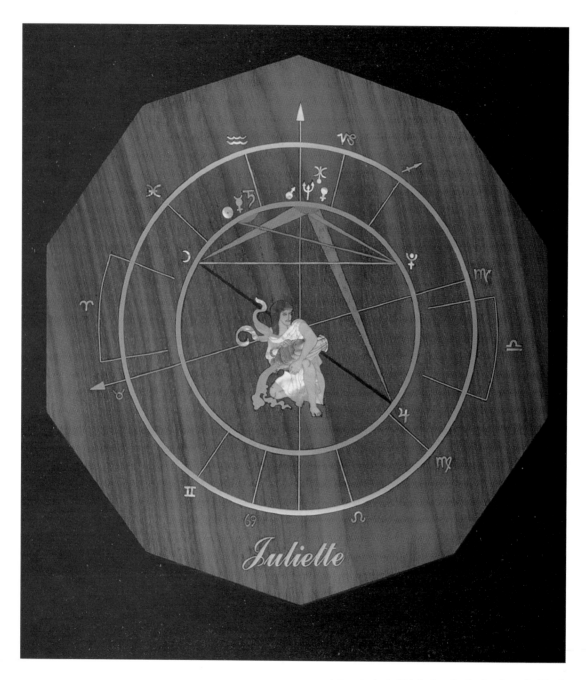

Juliette

▲ An astrological birth chart for the daughter of a friend.

✿ THE ART of INLAY

◄ An abalone macaw
for the Santa Cruz Guitar Co., 1993.
All feathers were cut separately
to make the most of light refraction.

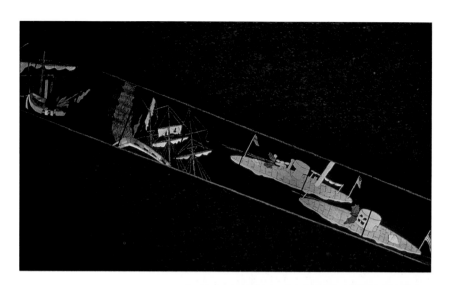

▶ ▲ Part of a Civil War set of banjos
for the Gibson Custom Shop, 1991.
Running the inlay over the truss rod cover
made a big difference in the overall look of the peghead.

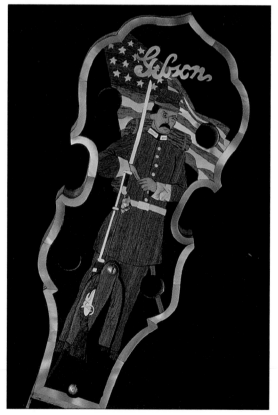

♣ THE ART of INLAY

◄ Sparrow inlaid in bubinga, 1984.
Four inches tall, abalone, ebony, mother-of-pearl, ivory,
and a turquoise eye.

▼ Hexagon box of rosewood
for housing a tourmaline crystal, 1992.
Wraparound inlay is a depiction of tourmaline
molecular structure. Sixty-three pink tourmalines, 9 zircons,
and three opals mark placement of specific elements.

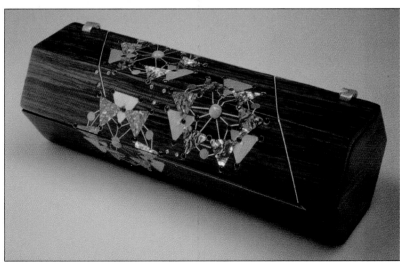

▲ "Tropical fish" for Gibson, 1992.

♣ THE ART of INLAY

▼ Currier and Ives, "The Life of a Hunter" resonator.

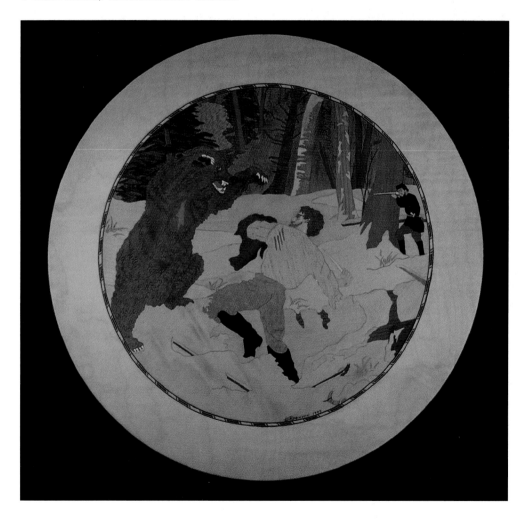

The parrot banjo was done as a commission for the Tsumura collection. It is a close, but not exact, copy of the inlays on an eighth-century Chinese *genkan* given to the Japanese emperor as a gift. The *genkan* is now a Japanese national treasure.

The stages shown in the construction of the parrot banjo resonator are as follows:

▶ 1. (top)
After the pieces of the inlay were cut, they were glued to pieces of the original drawings, then glued again to the spaces they would occupy on the ebony resonator.

▶ 2. (bottom)
The perimeters of the pieces have been scribed around, the pieces have been removed, and the scribe lines have been filled with chalk.

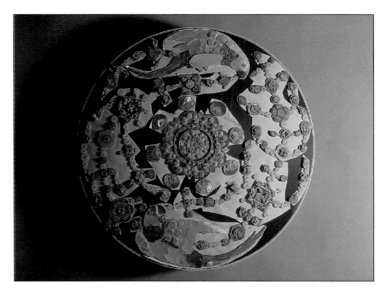

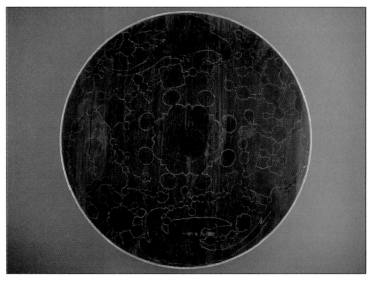

▲ 3. The completed inlay, before lacquering (top) and after lacquering (bottom).

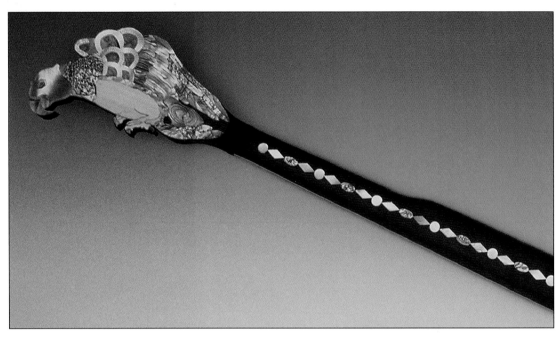

▲ ► The front and back
of the neck and peghead of the parrot banjo.

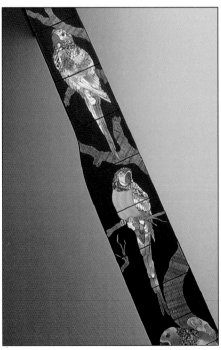

♣ THE ART *of* INLAY

Tack Gluing and Scribing

ONCE THE INLAY IS COMPLETELY CUT, it's time to fix it to the spot where it is to be inlaid. First the surface of the object to be decorated must be sanded completely smooth, down to 220 grit sandpaper.

Put a couple of dabs of model airplane glue or Duco Cement on the back of the inlay and press it onto the spot where it will be inlaid. Use only enough glue to hold it in place while you scribe around the perimeter with your X-ACTO knife.

Wait until the glue dries before attempting the scribing procedure. The lines don't have to be deep, but the top layers of grain must be sliced cleanly. If you use a needle or pointed scribe for this step, it will crush the grain instead of producing the desired clean line you are going to rout up next to. Trace around the perimeter of the inlay using the X-ACTO knife

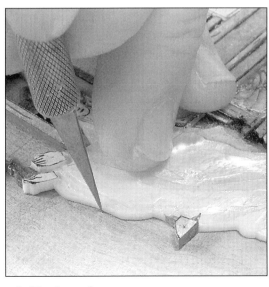

▲ Scribing the wood.

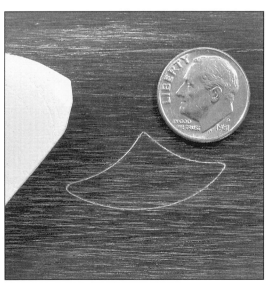

▲ A scribed line filled with chalk.

with a #11 blade, cutting the wood surface just deeply enough to leave a clean outline that will later be filled with chalk. Notice in the accompanying picture that my third and forth fingers are resting on the wood surface, in order to steady the blade while scribing.

After the scribing is completed, slip a single-edged razor blade under the inlay to pop it off the wood. Clean off the excess glue with the razor blade, and put the inlaid piece safely aside while you rub a piece of chalk over the scribed area. The chalk dust will fill in the lines, leaving an easily visible outline of the portion of the wood to be routed.

Routing

A WORD SHOULD BE SAID HERE about the relative ease of inlaying into darker woods compared to lighter ones, and harder woods as opposed to softer. Mistakes made during routing will be most obvious in light-colored woods like maple and birch. As far as the texture of the wood is concerned, you're much more likely to accidentally rout beyond the perimeter or blast out chunks in softer woods such as redwood and pine than in harder woods. Another advantage to using hard woods is that they hold up better during the final sandings than do soft woods, which are prone to sanding down faster than the hard inlay materials and could leave a dished surface around the artwork. For these reasons inlays are most often seen in hard dark woods such as ebony, walnut, and rosewood.

Should your inlay be composed of several types of materials such as shell, metal, and wood veneers, it will very likely be of different thicknesses to begin with. When the pieces are glued together on the metal scraper, the bottom surfaces will emerge fairly flush with one another, but the top surfaces will be of varying heights. When routing the cavity that the inlay is to be glued into, take care to cut only as deep as the thinnest inlay material.

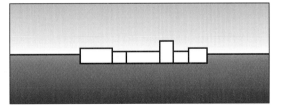

▼ Different inlay material heights in cavity.

If you rout too deeply, the thinnest pieces will be lower than the surface and the remaining paper and glue won't be sanded off afterward. If, in contrast, the routing is too shallow, you stand a chance of sanding entirely through the thinner pieces if they haven't been glued down tightly. Replacing a piece in an inlay that is already glued into the cavity is not for the faint of heart.

▲ Setting the router depth.

▼ The routing cavity
with the vacuum nozzle.

Fit your router with an appropriately sized bit and attach the router base to the body of the tool. If the inlay is large, use a bit that will take out a lot of wood in a short time, such as Dremel #650, #652, or #654. As you work out from the center toward the edges of the cavity, change to smaller bits to clean up nooks and crannies.

Some inlay artists like to begin routing at the perimeter and work toward the center, but I prefer to start in the center and work outward. That way I always have a level surface to rest the router base on, and the bit doesn't dig in deeper than it should.

Hold the thinnest piece of inlay material flush against the router base and adjust the bit to that depth. Next turn on your router and plunge it into the center of the cavity area and begin taking out the wood in widening strokes. Hold the handles on the base firmly, as the router may have a tendency to travel somewhere you don't want it to. Since this operation generates a lot of chips, I tuck the vacuum hose under my arm and position the nozzle near the router. If you can find a way to attach the nozzle directly to the router, that's fine too, but it may make maneuvering the tool somewhat awkward.

If your bit radius is too large as you get closer to the perimeter, change to a smaller one and rout excess wood until you see the last pieces flake off at the edge of the scribed line. You should be able to see the chalk in the groove at this time.

Clean up the perimeter and try to dry-fit the inlay at this time. Carefully rout out any areas that don't allow the inlay to fit flush in the cavity.

Gluing the Inlay into the Cavity

THIS STAGE OF THE GAME is fairly straightforward. Here again, I normally use cyanoacrylates, except for large banjo resonator plates, which have to be fussed with in the go-deck before the epoxy sets.

For a small inlay in a flat surface, put in just enough cyanoacrylate to cover the bottom of the cavity and press the inlay in until it hits bottom. Remember to have adequate ventilation when working with glues and epoxies. Next, apply glue around the perimeter until you see it fill flush and bead up higher than the surface. Let it dry and then repeat this process, because cyanoacrylate shrinks as it dries. Let it dry overnight before you try to level it, because if you attempt the sanding process prematurely, you might very well end up with a sticky mess.

When using epoxy, the procedure is basically the same, except that you should initially pour more of it into the cavity, spreading it evenly up to the edges. Apply a thin coat to the underside of the inlay before fitting it in. When you are ready to put the inlay in place, use light clamping pressure to ensure that you've stabilized it and press it in flush with the bottom of the cavity. The epoxy will bead out on its own and fill any remaining gaps, so you can eliminate the step of filling in the gaps from the top.

If you are inlaying into ebony you can minimize somewhat the visual effect of the gaps between the cavity and the inlay. Either use

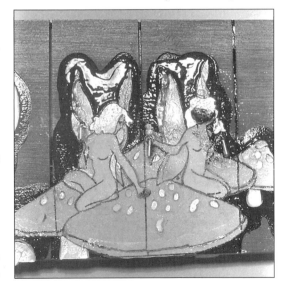

▼ Inlay with a bead of glue around the perimeter.

epoxy dyed with a carbon-based ink or mix some ebony dust with the epoxy, so that when the glue bleeds up to the surface the gaps are filled by the black mixture. The Locktite company also makes a black cyanoacrylate adhesive, for those of us who have found out the hard way that superglues can't be dyed by ordinary means. While this technique is a handy trick with ebony, it doesn't work with all woods. If you try this with the dust from other woods, you will probably get a mixture that doesn't match the surrounding wood after it dries and can even make the gap more obvious. Sometimes the mixture of epoxy and wood dust will prove to be too viscous and won't allow the inlay to seat flush on the bottom of the cavity. So bear this in mind while scribing and routing so your cavity will be as close to the inlay shape as possible.

It would be an unforgivable oversight for me not to recommend that you use the type of epoxy that requires a full 24 hours to dry as opposed to the "five-minute" type. There are two reasons that immediately come to mind. The first and most practical that you might need a little time to make sure you have the inlay precisely in the position you intend it to be in. The second is that if you've done a really good job, it's nice to think that your work might have a longer lifespan than you do. I can't count the times I've seen really good work in shambles only a few years after it was completed because someone had to hurry at the last stages of a project. If you're banking on longevity, the five-minute stuff just won't cut it.

In any event, you must be absolutely sure that the glue has dried completely before you attempt the leveling process.

Leveling

SECURE THE WORK TO A FLAT SURFACE. I usually use clamps for this, but you can use double-sided carpet tape if the underside of the piece is flat.

Make a wooden sanding block that fits in your hand. The commercial rubber ones are too soft and can leave the surface uneven after you've sanded it. My block has a flat surface of 4" by 1½" and is 2" tall. The upper edges are rounded over so it won't dig into my hand. With this size, a full sheet of sandpaper can be ripped into eight sections and folded comfortably around the flat surface one at a time, and gripped on the side of the block by my fingers and thumb.

Begin with 80 grit paper and sand with the grain of the wood the inlay sits in, vacuuming the dust as you go. Wear a mask as well because some dust always escapes at this point even with the vacuum on.

When the inlay is level with the wood surface, switch to 100 or 120 grit and clean off the 80 grit scratches. Next use 220 and 400 grit as the surface becomes smoother. You may want to sand 90 degrees to the direction you sanded with the previous grit, enabling you to see if you're getting all the scratches out. Make sure your final sanding is with the grain though, or the scratches will show under the finish.

There are "wet or dry" sandpapers that can be used with water, oil, or rubbing alcohol. They keep the sanding grit free of deposits longer and cut faster than dry sandpapers. These sandpapers work well for a job if your inlay doesn't have any light-colored veneers

▼ The sanding block position.

and is inlaid into a dense, tight-grained wood like ebony. Otherwise, wet dark-colored grit becomes embedded in your light veneers or in the open grain of walnut or padauk, and it is a nightmare to fix. Occasionally, I use 400 grit with oil to do a final brush up on an ebony fingerboard, but I usually take the extra time to use the dry sandpaper.

You must be particularly careful when sanding flush an inlay that has any metal in it. Metal heats up from the friction of the sanding and causes the glue to expand, which pushes the metal up higher. It's easy to sand through if you stay on one spot too long, so sand the metal a bit, move to another spot for awhile, and return to the metal after it's had a chance to cool down. Feel it with your palm or wrist to check if it's still warm.

Thin lines of bezel seem to work their way up quicker than larger flat sections of metal, so try to inlay them as flush as possible to begin with, so you won't have to sand them as much.

▶ Star map rosette built by Steve Klein for Dan Peek of the rock group America.

♣ THE ART of INLAY

Touchup

WHEN EVERYTHING IS LEVEL and sanded to 400 grit, vacuum out all excess dust and wipe the piece with a cloth. Look carefully for areas the glue didn't reach, or bubbles that need to be dug out with the razor knife and filled with glue again. Let them dry after regluing and sand them flush, starting with 220 grit.

If any pieces are sanded through or otherwise unacceptable, knock them out by routing most of the piece with the smallest bits and flicking out the edges with the razor knife. Cut a new piece and, after cleaning out the cavity to depth, glue the new one in.

Many times, if one piece is sanded through, the one next to it will be nearly sanded through also. Be careful not to sand through the second piece when releveling the first one, or you can end up chasing each sand-through until half your job needs replacing.

Engraving and Inking

MY INTENT IS NOT TO GIVE a complete explanation of the art of engraving, which would take a book in itself to treat adequately. There are already many excellent books and videos available detailing the process. However, I offer the following suggestions.

After your inlay is sanded to 400 grit and cleaned off, pencil on the detail lines. Lines on metal are best engraved using the graver with a chasing hammer. Engraving on shell and ivory is easier using the graver in both hands. I have found that I have much better control while engraving shell if I'm standing up and hovering directly over the inlay. While using the gravers and chasing hammer for metal, I always sit down with my arms resting on the tabletop and the inlay fastened down with clamps or double-sided tape.

Remember not to bear down very hard while engraving facial details in bone or ivory or you will leave wide, fuzzy-looking lines on the inlay. An X-ACTO blade can be used for these fine lines, but it will be difficult to control. Some people who prefer

▼ Engraving with a chasing hammer.

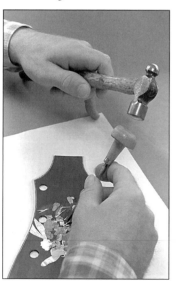

▼ Engraving by hand.

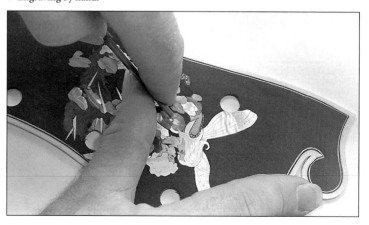

♣ THE ART of INLAY

scratching the lines with a diamond-point scribe obtain excellent results. I can say from experience that even the slightest amount of misdirected pressure on the graver can easily turn a smile into a smirk.

Lines in wood are easily done with a razor knife.

When the engraving is finished, the lines may be filled with colored inks, available from artist supply stores. To avoid color bleed in wood, you should seal it with a thin layer of lacquer after the lines have been engraved and before applying the inks. I use water-based inks and put them on the lines with a tiny paintbrush. When they're dry, the excess may be sanded off lightly with 400 or 600 grit sandpaper.

Some inlay artists use colored epoxies to fill the lines, or cyanoacrylate over the ink, but if a finish is to be put over the work, these steps aren't necessary.

These days my finish of choice is nitrocellulose lacquer, but I've completed many inlays that have had oil, wax, acrylic, or no finish at all. By the time you reach this stage, you may not want to mess with it anymore. However, a nicely executed finish can really bring out the highlights in your artwork and help to preserve it.

▼ Inking the engraved lines.

▼ A finished engraving.

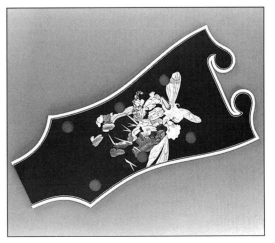

Epilogue

WITH ANY LUCK, I've kindled a desire in some readers to follow this craft where it might lead them. If so, my main purpose in writing this book will have been accomplished. With only a handful of people in America pursuing this craft, myriad opportunities are open for someone with an artistic eye and steady hands to create some beautiful inlaid images, and even make a living at it. Don't think that this book is the final word in the art of inlay, however. Learn these techniques but don't let them become a fossilized repertoire. Let them be a point of departure toward exploring new techniques and styles. Twenty years ago, if someone had told me I would be selling little puzzles made from shell and writing a book about it, I would have called them loco. So take a chance and surprise yourself....

Glossary

abalone. Any of a genus (*Haliotis*) of rock-clinging gastropod mollusks.

aliphatic resin. Yellow-colored wood glue made from open-chained organic compounds.

atsu-gai. Japanese term for thick-shell (.03"–.06") inlay.

bark. The tough flaky exterior of the shells or wood.

bench pin. Long wooden plate with a "V"-shaped slot in the end, used during the cutting process of inlay work.

bezel. Thin, flat rectangular length of metal, usually sold by the foot. Normally used in jewelry trade, specifically to wrap around stones and solder them in place. Used in inlaying when long, thin lines of metal are needed. It is inlaid so that the thin side is on the surface.

bird's beak. *See* **bench pin.**

bivalve. Having a shell composed of two distinct and, usually, movably articulated pieces.

book-match. Match of the grain of side by side pieces of wood or shell so they appear to be mirror images of each other.

bull's-eye. Section of air-hole in shell, grown over with more nacre. Also known as *fish-eye*.

burl. Section of wood with figure similar to closely packed bubbles and concentric circles.

burrs. Small rotary cutting tools.

CAD-CAM. Computer-assisted design-computer-assisted manufacturing.

cellulose. A polysaccharide of glucose units that constitutes the chief part of the cell wall of plants.

chasing hammer. Specially shaped hammer with a domed face and thin neck, used in engraving technique.

copyright. The exclusive legal right to reproduce, publish, and sell the matter and form of a literary, musical, or artistic work.

cyanoacrylate. Liquid acrylate monomer adhesive known for its quick setting time.

engraving. Forming shapes in a material by incising lines with metal tools.

flex-shaft. A type of router using a motor that is separated from the cutting tool by an encased flexible drive shaft.

focal length. The distance of a sharp focus from the surface of a lens.

frets. Metal ridges fixed at specific intervals on a stringed instrument fingerboard.

gastropod. Any of a large class Gastropoda of mollusks with a univalve shell or none and usually with a distinct head bearing sensory organs.

girdle. The widest part of a brilliant cut gem; the part usually grasped by the setting.

go-deck. A clamping device invented in Asia, consisting of a sturdy frame supporting a top and bottom plate and long dowels bent between the work and the top plate for clamping pressure.

grain. Stratification of wood fibers in a piece of wood.

gravers. Metal tools used to incise metal or shell in engraving work.

grit. In sandpaper, the number of grains of abrasive substance per square inch.

inlay. A type of decoration in which the artwork is fitted into a cavity and sanded flush with the surface.

kerf. The width of material a saw blade takes out as it cuts.

lacquer. Any of various clear or colored synthetic or natural organic coatings that dry to form a protective film.

lapidary. Of or relating to precious stones and the art of cutting them.

marquetry. Decorative technique whereby the artwork, usually veneer plates, is fixed directly to the surface of the workpiece, not in it, as with inlay.

Mohs' scale. A scale of hardness for minerals where *1* is talc and *10* is diamond.

mother-of-pearl. A specific family of bivalves.

nacre. The hard, pearly, iridescent substance forming the inner layer of a mollusk shell.

needle files. Miniature files used to reach hard-to-get areas.

open grain. Pits in wood surface caused by diversion of wood fibers.

paua. Type of abalone shell from New Zealand.

pressure-dyed veneer. Wood veneer artificially colored in a pressure cooker.

refraction. Deflection from a straight path undergone by a light ray in passing obliquely from one medium into another in which its velocity is different.

resonator. Large, lipped plate attached to the back of a banjo to reflect sound waves forward.

router. A machine with a revolving vertical spindle and cutter for milling out the surface of wood or metal.

scribe. A sharp pointed tool for making marks on wood, metal, or shell.

shank. The end of a cutting tool that is gripped in a chuck.

slabbing. The act of cutting long, flat plates of shell for inlaying purposes.

tack gluing. Putting a minimal amount of glue on the back of an inlay so it may be scribed around without moving but easily lifted off afterward.

tagua. A nut from a palm fruit used sometimes as a substitute for ivory.

tarsia certosina. Italian term for inlaying wood veneers in wood panels.

usu-gai. Japanese for "thin-shell," referring to shell around .005" thick, which is cut into patterns and glued directly to a lacquered undercoat. A finish is then built up to the level of the shell and buffed.

V-block. *See* **bench pin.**

veneer. Thin sheet of wood, usually $\frac{1}{28}$" or $\frac{1}{40}$" thick.

vertex. Point of an angle where two lines intersect.

viscosity. I like to think of this as the ability or inability of a liquid to flow, i.e., molasses has a higher viscosity than water. But the dictionary says "the ratio of the tangential frictional force per unit area to the velocity gradient perpendicular to the direction of flow of a liquid."

Suggestions for Further Reading

Marquetry by Pierre Raymond (translated from French edition), Taunton Press, 1989.

Pearls by Kristin Joyce and Shellei Addison, Simon & Schuster, 1993.

Fine Woodworking on Marquetry and Veneer, Taunton Press, 1987.

The Art of Engraving by James B. Meek, Brownell & Son, 1984.

Art Nouveau Furniture by Alastair Duncan, Clarkson N. Potter, Inc., 1982.

Raden by H. Arakawa (in Japanese, but excellent photos).

Suppliers

Tools:

Any competent jeweler's supply or lapidary outlet should be able to outfit you with any of the tools I've mentioned in this book. Hardware stores will probably carry Dremel tools, X-ACTO knives, spring clamps, glues, epoxies, and files. If you still can't find what you need, try:

Rio Grande Albuquerque
6901 Washington N.E.
Albuquerque, NM 87109
phone: (800) 545-6566
http://www.riogrande.com

Veneers:

West Friendship Hardwoods
Box 103
West Friendship, MD 21794

The Woodworker's Store
(catalog)
21801 Industrial Blvd.
Rogers, MN 55374-9514
phone: (612) 428-2199
fax: (612) 428-8668

Constantine's
2050 Eastchester Rd.
Bronx, NY 10461
phone: (800) 223-8087
http://www.constantines.com

Inlay Materials:

There are several suppliers of shell in the United States. Some buy their shell from other sources listed here. Shop around to get your best deal.

**Chuck Erikson
(the Duke of Pearl)**
(Distributes a good catalogue and knows his stuff. He also supplies fossil ivory and other goodies.)
18072 Greenhorn Rd.
Grass Valley, CA 95945
phone/fax: (530) 273-4116

Len Wood/Custom Guitar Shop
21265 Steven's Creek Blvd., #205-6
Cupertino, CA 95014-5715
phone: (408) 257-6829

Swank Shell Inlay (catalog)
7 Tenby Court
Waldorf, MD 20602
phone: (301) 843-2192

Luthier's Mercantile
(catalog for stringed instrument makers)
P.O. Box 774
Healdsburg, CA 95448
phone: (800) 477-4437
http://www.lmii.com

**Stewart MacDonald's
Guitar Shop Supply** (catalog)
21 N. Shafer St. or Box 900
Athens, OH 45701
phone: (800) 848-2273
fax: (614) 593-7922
http://www.stewmac.com

Masecraft Supply
(reconstituted stone, bone, plastics, shell laminates)
Box 423
Meriden, CT 06450
phone: (800) 682-5489

About the Author

Larry Robinson is a self-taught inlay artist of world-class stature. He began using hand tools in his father's workshop at age six, and was making furniture with power tools by age 11. Years later, while studying classical guitar, he hired a luthier to build a custom acoustic. Seeing no progress, however, Robinson eventually "wormed my way into his shop and built the whole guitar myself." He was subsequently offered an apprenticeship by the luthier.

Robinson's introduction to inlay was three years later, in 1975. Working at Alembic, Inc., he accidentally drilled a hole through a $2,000 electric bass while installing a pickup. "As I mentally started looking for a new job, I called my boss over and showed him what I'd done. He shrugged and said, 'Just put an inlay over it.'" Robinson quickly learned the basics of the process, and soon became a specialist in the art.

Today he is a recognized expert whose decorative inlays grace instruments, boxes, wall hangings, lap desks, and various objets d'art. His musical clients include such names as Stanley Clarke, John Entwistle, Jerry Garcia, David Grisman, Paul Kantner, Greg Lake, Fleetwood Mac, Hot Tuna, Led Zeppelin, and many others. He has numerous inlaid pieces in the Tsumura Collection and other prized collections in the U.S. and England, and his work has appeared in *Guitar Player, Fine Woodworking,* and *Folk Harp Journal* magazines, the *Gibson Custom Shop Calendar,* and the books *Pearls* and *Acoustic Guitars and Other Fretted Instruments.*

Art of Inlay is Robinson's first book. He lives in Sonoma County, California, with his wife, Connie, and two daughters. Visit his Web site at *http://robinsoninlays.com.*

▲ Photo by Frances Robinson

About the Photographer

Richard Lloyd has been photographing artwork professionally since 1984. He lives in Tahlequah, Oklahoma, with his wife, two daughters, and a zillion pets.

BOOK & JACKET DESIGN BY

GEORGE MATTINGLY DESIGN, BERKELEY

USING ROBERT SLIMBACH'S MINION & MATTHEW CARTER'S SOPHIA TYPEFACES.